GO KART RACING - CHASSIS SETUP

A Complete Guide To A Better Handling Kart

by Brian Martin

PRINTED IN U.S.A.

Published by

MARTIN MOTORSPORTS

P.O.Box 12654   Ft. Wayne, Ind. 46864

The Unfair Advantage

Mark Dohanue said in his book "The Unfair Advantage", preparation is the unfair advantage. When Mark teamed with Roger Penske in the early sixties, they took a lowly AMC Javelin and put it on top of the heap in SCCA racing. Their persistence and meticulous attention to detail lead to their winning the 1971 Trans-AM championship. They went on to score wins in the prestigious Can-Am series, and finally winning the 1972 Indy 500. During this time they developed many of the procedures that Penske still uses today to make his Indy team so successful. Mark and Roger proved that making the chassis work for you instead of against you, can make you a winner.

Everyone in the race wants to win just as much as you do. Unfortunately only one person gets to. To get the edge on the competition you must make that extra effort. Proper prepartion does not end with wiping the dirt off and changing gears between race dates. Proper preparation means striving to make your kart handle as well as possible race after race. NASCAR drivers spend many hours practicing the week before a race. We know that people like Dale Earnhardt and Terry Labonte aren't out there to learn how to drive. The real reason, is to improve the handling of the chassis. If handling is important to them it's important to us.

Every karter I know is looking for that rocket motor that will make him or her a winner. To be honest, there just isn't that much difference between stock engines. Every once in a while you run across an engine that just seems to be a little quicker, but for the most part, Blue printed engines are not that much different from one another. What this means is that if you want to win you need to find the speed somewhere else and that somewhere else is kart handling.

This book contains a wide range of basic information, all presented to help you better understand how a chassis works and what you can do to improve its handling characteristics. There is a lot of valuable information whether you are assembling a new kart, rebuilding a old kart, or just trying to fine tune your chassis. The end result is, you will go faster, be more competitive, and have more fun doing it.

TABLE OF CONTENTS

We have attempted to present the best information available as accurately as possible. Most of the information has evolved from years of racing. Not everything presented may be for you. It is the responsibility of each karter to determine his own requirements. It is also the karters responsibility to stay within the sprit and intent of the rules of the organization in which he will be participating. No responsibility or liability can be accepted by the author or Martin Motorsports for any personal injury or mechanical damage sustained as a result of the information contained in this book.

THE MARTIN MOTORSPORTS GUARANTEE

If you are not completely satisfied with the purchase of this book. Return it with your sales receipt, prepaid, and we will refund the full purchase price.

Introduction

What really separates a winner from a runner up? Is two things. One, the driver and two, doing the preparation necessary to make a kart handle it's very best every race.

The driver is the single most important variable in kart handling. Drivers come in various sizes and weights and have completely different driving styles. A kart setup for one driver may handle terrible for another. I would like to think that if a kart is setup properly anybody could drive it and be fast, but I'm not sure that that's true. On any given day, every thing has to be just right to get the maximum out of the kart. The driver has to be mentally sharp and alert the whole race, hit every apex just right, and read the signs as to what to do next, and above all be smooth. The driver is the thing that melds everything together into that winning combination.

Proper kart preparation is an on going thing. You should, for the most part, disregard what other drivers are doing. There are so many variables in making a kart handle properly, it's almost impossible to copy someone else's setup and have it work for you. You must think for yourself and use your own testing plan and judgement to tune your chassis for peak performance. The better you understand the elements that affect a kart's handling, the quicker you will be able to dial in the kart at any given track. The important thing is to find out what it takes to make your kart as fast as possible.

The new frames on the market today are really nice. They are designed with a lot of experience in them, which makes them easy to setup, but it doesn't take a new kart to win. With the proper time and effort, almost any frame can get you into the winner's circle.

I was at a speedway race, and while walking through the pits I noticed a 15 year old Margay. It looked a little out of place as it didn't have a great deal of farings and the driver set almost straight up. I immediately thought he was outclassed and was probably only there for the fun of it. In talking to him, he said the kart had always handled very well, so he didn't feel it necessary to buy a new one. Well, when the race started he went right to the front and ran in the top three the whole race. Yes, he probably had a good motor too, but he had to go through the tech barn just like everyone else. What set him apart was how smooth he could maneuver around the track. This just goes to prove almost any frame can win with the right combination.

I think it is best to understand how a rolling chassis functions before you plunge into changing the setup on your kart. I have put the chapters covering theory first, Chassis, Tires, and Aerodymanics. These chapters deal with all the basic concepts it takes to make a kart handle. You don't have to completely understand all the information, in fact some of it may not become clear until you apply the theory to your own kart.

The chapter Initial Chassis Setup, will tell you how to establish a baseline for your kart. It encludes a procedure on how to measure up your chassis to find out what you have. With all the adjustable componets on some of the newer frames it's easy to get things out of kelter. A baseline is necessary so you can always get back to a known starting point. It also includes a procedure to get you from a bare frame to a rolling chassis.

The Trackside chapter helps you fine tune the chassis to your driving style. It will also help you sort out oversteer and understeer problems which may occur at the track because of such things as weather.

The chapter on Dirt Tracks covers reading the track, adjusting the kart for track conditions and Dirt Track Driving Techniques.

This book covers the principles involved in good handling as it relates to any kart. However, not all karts are alike. Some karts are better suited for dirt tracks than road courses. This is usually evident by the degree of caster on the front spindle. Most true dirt karts have spindles that are adjustable from the drivers seat. More and more dirt karts are mounting the engine behind the driver to get more left side weight. The desire for more left side weight on speedway and indoor tracks has lead to the development of LTO (Left Turn Only) and the offset chassis.

If you look around at the track you will see several different types and lengths of exhaust pipes, a lot of different gear combinations, and different spindle settings, everybody does things just a little bit different. This should tell you there is no magic or secret formulas. This book doesn't have all the answers but it will help you find the setup that will work best for you.

The perfect setup is a fleeting thing. What works good today can be off next week. Things are always changing, outside temperature, hardness of the tires, tire air pressure, frame stress, and even the drivers attitude can all effect performance. The idea or objective should be to obtain a reasonably good initial setup or baseline, so you can fine tune the chassis on race day with a mininum of effort. Ideally on race day you would like to keep adjustments down to changing tire air pressure on pavement tracks and tire stagger or compound on dirt tracks. Remember the original intent is to have fun, not to work your fanny off all day. I hope this book will help you have a more enjoyable race day.

CHASSIS THEORY

The frame, or chassis as it is sometimes called, is the heart of the system. Getting the frame to work for you, not against you has been the goal of racers for years. In this chapter we will discuss frames, frame flex and most of the components which turn the frame into a rolling chassis.

In kart racing the frame assumes a more important role than it does in stock cars because we have no real suspension parts. Things like kingpin inclination and caster are built into most karts. The biggest variable of all is frame flex, which can be good or bad depending on your driving style.

FRAME CONSTRUCTION

Ten, fifteen years ago the majority of all karts on the market were fairly stiff, but the trend in recent years has been to more and more flexible frames. All the newer frames flex in the corners. The frame is in effect one long torsion bar, or perhaps more correctly many small ones welded together. The effect of all these stress members and their interaction is mind boggling.

I feel some flexibility is good, and even makes the kart setup a bit easier, but I have some concern, with some of the newer frames, that over time the frame may not rebound back to its original condition. A few of the newer frames have very small center sections which are subjected to terrific stress over the racing season. While this may not be a concern for someone who buys a new kart every year, those of us who are financially unable to do that, want a kart which will be stable over a three to five year period. Unfortunately we won't know if the new karts will last this long for a few more years. At a recent seminar, a major chassis builder said current frames are only good for about 18 months and then should be replaced. Looking at some of the chassis on the market today I can believe that. It's really a scary thing to think we are building in planned obsolescence for such a high dollar item. A thing like that makes me glad I don't have to compete on a national level.

If you race the same track week after week, a frame can take a set which in effect diminishes its flexibility. If this is true of your race schedule, it's a good idea to take at least one practice day each year and run several laps in a backward direction.

1

This will help alleviate this condition somewhat. We will discuss this condition in a little more detail in the setup section.

When discussing kart handling one term we have heard little about is side bite. Side bite is a term that means the ability of the kart to stay stuck to the track, without sliding, when going around a corner. When you drive a kart on asphalt, sliding around a corner is not as fast as driving around a corner, so we want a kart that has good side bite. If you have the correct amount of side bite the kart will unload the inside rear tire when you negotiate a corner which will reduce the harmful effects of scrubbing the tire. Too much side bite can make a kart hop or bicycle around a corner, or it can cause you to scrub off so much speed the engine will bog down because it's out of its power band. Too little side bite will cause the kart to be loose. The same effect as driving on a wet track.

If you do any dirt racing you will find that in the stock classes you'll want less bite in the rear, we want the front end to stay put, while the back end of the kart is set on the loose side, sliding slightly so we can keep the RPM up in the corners. For the 2-cycle classes you can use more rear side bite to help pull out of the corners. Side bite on entry is not a concern because you will hopefully be putting the kart in a power slide.

The design of the kart frame itself has a lot to do with how much side bite you will have. A good indication of what you can expect is to measure the width of the rear frame rails. The narrower the rails the more rear side bite the frame is likely to have. A narrow kart would measure 24" to 25" while a wider kart would measure 27" to 28" measured at the center of the frame rails. The front end width is measured the same way. Typically on a narrow kart the front will measure 22" to 24", a wide kart 28" or 30". This is measured from kingpin to kingpin. Karts with a narrow distance between kingpins will have more front end bite.

Side bite is also effected by frame stiffness. The frame is essentially a series of torsions bars welded together. The shorter the bars, the more triangulation, the stiffer the frame. Long bars with fewer cross members means more flex. The frame stiffness will to some extent control which tires will

work best on your kart. If you are running in a class which has a tire rule, the required tire is probably a Burris M15 which is a harder compound for longer life. In this case you want a narrower front end, this will help heat up the front tires quicker. The rear end could be wide or narrow. The narrow rear end would give us a kart that will bite pretty well and probably would lift the inside wheels. You could also run the wide rear and move the rear wheels in tight until you get just the lift you want, this would be the most desirable situation.

Dirt drivers might also choose the narrower front end and standard rear end, to let the front end stay put while the rear end is a little looser to keep the engine from bogging. Front end bite is very important for dirt racing.

The frames flexibility can be seen on the scales. By using the "17 degree method" you will need to scale the kart with the flex set in a loose condition and then again with the flex set tight. You should be able to note the variations in the amount of weight transferred. This is more fully explained in the chapter called Initial Setup.

I guess the unanswered question here is do you want a flexible kart or not? If you had a chassis with no flex at all, what would happen? Depending on the tires a couple of things will happen. With hard low traction tires the centrifugal force and weight transfer would probably cause both ends to break loose, even at a relatively slow speed and you would have trouble keeping the kart on the track. With high traction tires, with lots of bite, you would soon find yourself up on two wheels bicycling around the turn. One other thing to consider here is that the chassis is not the only thing that flexes. The side walls of the tires will also flex. If the side wall flexes enough, or should I say too much, it will distort the foot print of the tire and control of the kart will be lost.

Some flex in the frame is desirable, but it is best to keep it to a minimum, just enough to balance out the static weight balance. If the frame flexes just a bit it will settle down on the tires, without distorting the tire patch, improving tire bite. Generally, low horsepower classes want a more flexible kart, while 2-cycle and high horsepower 4-cycle classes prefer a stiffer frame.

TORSION BARS

Your first inclination may be to say that we don't have torsion bars on karts. You would be very wrong in this statement. There are several potential torsion bars on a kart and in almost all cases they will cause you more harm than good.

A true torsion bar is a spring in the form of a tube of steel, either solid or hollow, that is held fixed at one end and allowed to twist at the other end. Naturally, it resists being twisted and tries to rebound to its original shape. This is what gives it its springing action. Almost any bar has some degree of twist before it bends. Some have more give than others.

As a bar is twisted it tries harder and harder to lift the other end. How tight a bar can be twisted depends on its size, length, and the material it's made of.

A simplified example of how a torsion bar works would be a popsicle stick. If you hold one end rigid and twist the other end you can feel the increasing pressure on the fixed end as it tries to move. Now let's assume the popsicle stick is a cross member or a nerf bar. If the bar is mounted

I have a real concern about this type of construction. This type of frame has lots of flex, but does it always return back to the baseline? What happens in a accident? If you are considering buying one used I would recomend taking it for a test session first just to check it out.

Many of the karts on the market today employ an adjustable rear torsion bar. This bar is set vertical for maximum stiffness.

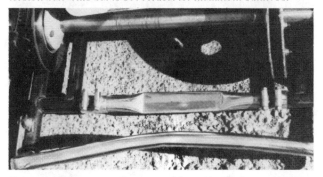

This kart has its rear torsion bar positioned for minimum stiffness.

loose it will exert little or no pressure. If it's mounted rigid and one end is twisted or flexed, it will exert a great amount of pressure on the other end.

As a kart corners the frame flexes by twisting or winding up the frame rail torsion bars. The amount of flex is determined by the combination of all the torsion bars. Generally speaking, the longer and less supported the rails are the more flexible the frame will be. A frame with short triangulated rails will have less flex.

Many of the karts on the market today employ an adjustable rear torsion bar. The rear torsion bar works on a very simple principle. The center of the tube has a flat section which is the important part of the tube. When the flat section is mounted horizontal the side rails can flex somewhat independent of each other. When the flat section is mounted vertical almost all flex is removed from the bar and it acts to stiffen up the rear end.

Most of us prefer the frame have some flex, so it's necessary to use some caution when setting up the kart to avoid making it too tight. The biggest offenders in this area are long nerf bars or side rails. When mounting these they must be mounted with rubber and/or spring shock mounts. The nerf bar mounting holes must align with the kart mounting

3

holes without putting undue pressure on the rail. If the nerf bars are mounted rigid to the frame they will reduce flex.

Another potential torsion bar is the front and rear bumpers. The mounting arms should be pre-bent so they align with the kart mounting tabs without any pressure applied. If the bars are damaged in an accident you should unbolt them and insure they are not stressing the frame.

This kart will have Ackerman steering because the tie-rod bolts will travel different distances around the steering circle.

ACKERMAN STEERING

Ackerman steering is where the inside front wheel is steered in a sharper arc than the outside front wheel. The reason for doing this is to eliminate the scrubbing the inside tire would have to do if it was turning the same radius as the outside front tire. On large open tracks with sweeping turns this scrubbing is very small an is of little consequence. On short tight tracks such as an oval, scrubbing becomes more of a concern.

Most of the karts in use today have the Ackerman set at zero. This means if you turn the steering wheel 15 degrees, both front wheels will move an equal number of degrees. In most cases, about 7 to 9 degrees. The actual number depends on the placement of the tie-rod mounting holes. If you had Ackerman dialed into the kart the outside wheel would turn 7 degrees and the inside wheel would turn 12 degrees.

This kart will have "0" Ackerman because the tie-rods are mounted with a single bolt. Both spindles will move an equal distance when the steering shaft is rotated.

You can tell if you have Ackerman by looking for two things. First the tie-rods will be connected together with one bolt (Single Point Steering) at the bottom of the steering column, and second, the tie-rods will be connected to the spindle arm the same distance from the kingpin on both sides. If both spindles are the same and you have single point steering, the Ackerman will be zero.

Ackerman can be added to a kart in two ways. The correct way is by changing the steering shaft to one that has multiple connecting points. The most

The adjustment holes in this spindle arm serves two purposes. If the tie-rods on both sides are moved closer to the kingpin bolt the steering will be quicker. If the tie-rod end on just one side is moved there will be a Arkerman effect for a turn in that direction only. There will be reverse Arkerman for a turn in the opposite direction.

common of these is a Vee pattern which in itself is non-adjustable. It gives you the same Ackerman effect in both left and right turns which is the desired effect. If you turn the steering wheel 15 degrees left it will turn the right front wheel 7 degrees and the left front wheel 12 degrees. If the turn is sharper the Ackerman effect increases.

The second less desirable method of adjusting Ackerman is to move one of the tie-rod ends on the spindle in closer to the kingpin. The problem with this is, you only have Ackerman when turning in the direction of that wheel. You will have reverse Ackerman when you turn the opposite direction. You should not use this on a road course, but you may want to use it on an oval.

A couple of other points of note in connection with Ackerman. If you move both tie-rod ends closer to the kingpins they will offset each other and Ackerman will still be zero. Moving both ends closer will decrease the number of degrees the wheels turn per degrees the steering wheel is turned, so the steering will feel quicker but Ackerman itself is unchanged. Tie-rod length has no effect on Ackerman.

Using Ackerman is a decision you will have to make depending on the type of racing you are participating in. If you use is, it's best to stick with a fixed amount. I think Dr. Dick Berggren said it best, "Ackerman is something to talk about but not to adjust".

KINGPIN INCLINATION

The kingpin is the pivot around which the spindle rotates to steer the wheel. The kingpin inclination is the angle between the kingpin axis and a true vertical line where the kingpin axis line hits the ground. It is best viewed by looking at the spindle from the front of the kart. Refer to Fig. 1. Do not confuse kingpin inclination with caster, which is best viewed from the side of the kart. Kingpin inclination is designed into the spindle bracket and it is not adjustable on most karts.

In the last few years the amount of kingpin inclination has been decreased somewhat. Some karts such as the Margay have an off center washer called a pill which fits in the spindle bracket. This allows the inclination to be adjusted a few degrees. Most karts built in the last few years have a kingpin inclination of 12 or 15 degrees. On some of the

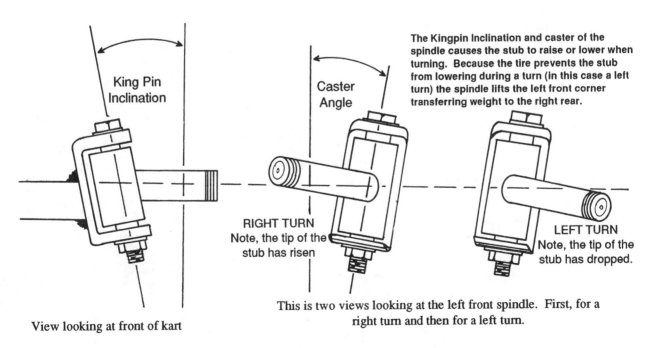

The Kingpin Inclination and caster of the spindle causes the stub to raise or lower when turning. Because the tire prevents the stub from lowering during a turn (in this case a left turn) the spindle lifts the left front corner transferring weight to the right rear.

King Pin Inclination

Caster Angle

RIGHT TURN
Note, the tip of the stub has risen

LEFT TURN
Note, the tip of the stub has dropped.

View looking at front of kart

This is two views looking at the left front spindle. First, for a right turn and then for a left turn.

Figure 5, How the spindle transfers weight.

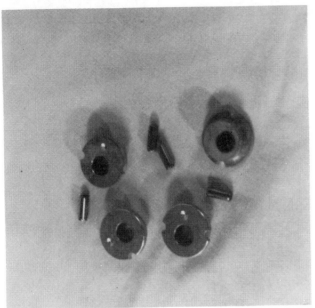

Offset washers, sometimes called caster pills, such as these can be used to adjust Kingpin Inclination as well as caster.

SPINDLES

The spindle works together with the kingpin inclination to get the kart around a turn. The spindle is where all the action is. Before we get too involved in how the spindle works we need to cover a few points of how it is constructed. The spindle which pivots on the kingpin axis must give us a flat horizontal shaft on which to mount the tire and wheel assembly. This shaft is often referred to as the spindle stub. The bracket that the tie-rod is mounted on is referred to as the spindle arm.

Looking at Fig. 1 you can see that the spindle axis must match the kingpin axis if the wheel is to remain flat. Spindles can be purchased for different degrees of kingpin inclination, 12 and 15 degrees being the most common. If the spindles are not matched to the kingpin inclination the tire camber (which we will discuss later) will be incorrect.

Here is how the spindle/kingpin inclination combination works. Refer to Fig. 1. Turning the wheels as in making a turn to the left or right rotates the spindle around the kingpin axis. Because the kingpin axis is inclined, the path of the wheel is not

newer karts on the market this angle has been reduced. The optimum angle occurs when the line drawn through the center of the kingpin intersects a vertical line drawn through the center of the wheel at the point of track contact. This provides single point steering by bring the center of the wheels rotating plane on the centerline of the kingpin. However, on most karts this is not achieved. The kingpin axis is always inside of the centerline of the tire. This causes scrub radius, which is more fully explained later.

Most karters don't buy a kart based on kingpin inclination. We usually have to make the best of what we have. It's easier to adjust our driving style for too much inclination than not enough. You need to get the front wheels pointed straight as soon as possible coming out of the turns. The more inclination you have, the harder it is to push the kart forward while the wheels are turned. The drag produced by the angled wheels is similiar to having front wheel brakes. You can verify this by pushing your kart in a straight line and then turning the wheels. You will notice immediately that the kart becomes difficult to push.

The kingpin inclination must be the same on both sides, if not you may experience a hard pull to one side under hard braking. For dirt racing this could be used to help pull the kart down into the corners, but this is a very delicate balance.

The kingpin inclination an or camber on this wheel is of questionable benefit. Can you imagine the position the kart would need to be in for the tire patch to be flat. The driver said it was that way when he bought the kart and he didn't know what to do with it so he didn't do anything.

This spindle is adjustable for caster and camber by use of the off-set washers retaining the kingpin. Note the four small holes in the top washer. Each position is a different setting.

was vertical the kart weight would tend to be located near the inside edge of the tire. I suspect with the current popularity of karting we will see manufacturers doing more research in this area.

SCRUB RADIUS

An important term that comes into play with kingpin inclination, although you don't hear much about it in kart racing, is scrub radius. To picture what the scrub radius is refer to Fig. 2. Imagine the kingpin axis line projected all the way down to the ground. Now picture the centerline of the tire contact patch. The distance which exists between the kingpin axis line and the tire centerline is the scrub radius.

The length of the scrub radius varies greatly depending on three things. The tread width of the tire, the amount of wheel offset and the kingpin inclination. When the wheel is steered, the tire actually rotates on this scrub radius. It is desirable to have the smallest possible scrub radius.

flat or level. For our example lets use the left front spindle, looking at it from the left side of the kart with the tire removed. If the steering wheel is turned to the left as for a left turn, you will note that the tip of the spindle drops down. The actual amount it drops will depend on kingpin inclination and the length of the spindle. When a wheel and tire are mounted on the spindle, it can not drop, so the left front corner of the kart must raise up. Depending on the amount of flex in the kart frame, the right front wheel may lift off the ground. Another thing this is doing is transferring weight to the right rear.

I'm sure you've noticed that if you turn the wheels and then take your hands off the steering wheel the front wheels will attempt to return to the straight ahead position. This is because the weight of the kart is pushing down on the raised spindle. This same force pushing down on the spindle will resist any force tending to turn them in the first place. This is one of the reasons some of the newer karts are experimenting with less kingpin inclination.

Kingpin inclination has two advantages, the first and perhaps the main reason it's used is because of the stability it gives to the kart when driving in a straight line. The second, is that the weight carried on the spindle is more evenly distributed across the spindle bolt. If the kingpin axis

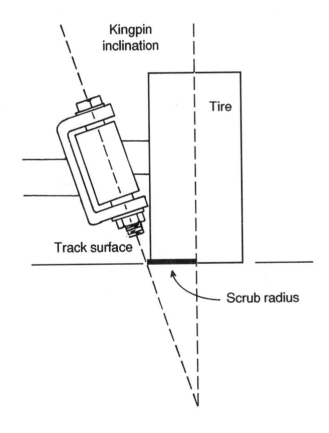

Figure 2. Scrub Radius

7

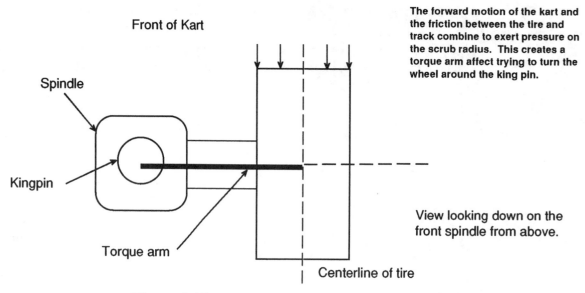

Front of Kart

Spindle

Kingpin

Torque arm

Centerline of tire

The forward motion of the kart and the friction between the tire and track combine to exert pressure on the scrub radius. This creates a torque arm affect trying to turn the wheel around the king pin.

View looking down on the front spindle from above.

Figure 3. The torque arm caused by the scrub radius.

During forward travel of the kart the scrub radius acts as a torque arm which is trying to rotate around the kingpin axis because of the road friction on the contact patch. This in effect is adding toe-out to the front end. With a small scrub radius, little static toe-in is required to compensate for the toe-out. If the wheel is moved out by use of a larger offset, or an extra long spindle stub, the scrub radius can become a sufficient torque arm requiring considerable static toe-in to offset the toe-out developed when speeding down the straight. I do not know how prominent this is in karting. However, this will give you a good example of what can happen. Fortunately we do not have as much slop in our front end componets , or should not have, as stock cars do.

Another effect of the scrub radius is the weight transfer we discussed in kingpin inclination. Offset wheel spacing or extended spindle stubs will cause the stub to drop lower during cornering, transferring more weight. In turn it will also cause the steering to be more difficult.

This kart has a very large scrub radius. However, the driver is quite happy with it, and is winning races. It could prove the text books aren't always right. But just maybe if the tire was moved in and the kart readjusted it would be even faster.

An example of a zero scrub radius spindle. Note the kingpin is mounted inside of the wheel. While technically more correct, zero scrub radius spindles have shown no real advantage in kart racing.

There are a few karts on the market which have "O" scrub radius. Technically "O" scrub radius is best because it has no torque arm pushing on the spindle. However, in kart racing, these karts haven't exhibited any real advantage. Part of the reason may be that a "O" scrub radius spindle transfers less weight.

This is another view of zero scrub radius.

CASTER

Caster provides the kart with directional stability. Directional stability is the ability of the kart to travel straight ahead with a minimum of steering corrections by the driver.

Caster can be viewed by removing a front wheel and looking at the spindle from the side. Caster should always be positive. Positive caster is defined as when the top of the kingpin is tipped to the rear of the kart. Caster is measured in degrees from a true vertical line in relationship to a line drawn through the center of the spindle. Refer to Fig. 4.

The basic principle of how caster works has been used for hundreds of years on such things as furniture casters and shopping carts. The wheel pivot point is mounted ahead of the wheel so that whenever the pivot is driven, the wheel will trail

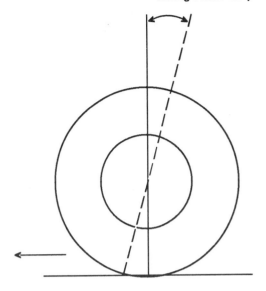

Caster angle. Note the center line of the tire is following behind the pivot.

Figure 4. Caster angle

along behind. You cannot push the wheel out in front of the pivot point because it will always swivel around behind.

This same principle applies to a kart, except on a kart the wheel cannot really swivel. If the spindle is tilted backward at the top, positive camber, the projected centerline of the pivot strikes the ground

Caster on this kart is adjustable by rotating the spindle assembly. Note the marks scribed on the spindle bracket and the frame. The kingpin can also be raised and lowered.

ahead of the tire contact patch. When the kart is driven forward, the pivot drags the wheel behind it giving the kart directional stability. This produces an automatic steering effect and the front wheels tend to align themselves with the direction in which the kart is going.

Caster is adjustable on several of the newer karts. So the question becomes, where do you set it? Generally, it is best to start with about 15 degrees of caster and work forward in one or two degree steps. For pavement racing with turns in both directions, left and right caster should be set the same. If it isn't you will have caster stagger.

CASTER STAGGER

Caster stagger has been unadjustable until only recently. Some of the newer karts now allow this to be adjusted. Caster stagger is something you would not want to adjust until you have the kart handling pretty much the way you want it.

Caster stagger is when we have more positive caster in the right front than in the left front. The reason for using caster stagger is to help the wheels steer themselves into the left hand corners. For short track racing where there is virtually no straightaways, you can use as much as four degrees. The drawback of using too much caster stagger is the increased effort in turning the steering wheel

You don't see many karts setup this way. Note wear on the inside edges of the tires. This could be the result of camber or kingpin inclination or both. I would not recomemd you set your kart up this way.

back over to the right to correct for oversteer, which is often done in dirt racing. The greater the caster stagger, the greater the effort required to turn the wheel back past the straight ahead centerline of the steering wheel.

The higher the speed of the race track, the less caster stagger you should use. The amount of caster stagger is totally up to the driver's preference and several settings should be tried before the final setting is arrived at.

CAMBER

Camber is defined as the inward or outward tilt of the wheel at the top when compared with a true vertical line drawn through the centerline of the tire. This is best viewed from the front of the kart. If the top of the wheel tilts out or away from the kart the camber is positive. If the top of the wheel tilts inward toward the kart, the camber is negative. The amount the wheel is tilted away from the vertical center line is measured in degrees.

Camber is not adjustable on most karts. The camber angle is controlled by the angle that the spindle stub is welded on the spindle. The camber can only be changed by changing the kingpin inclination, or rewelding the spindle stub.

Some karts, such as the Margay, have an off center washer called a pill which fits into the spindle bracket, which allows the camber to be adjusted a few degrees. Camber can be changed by buying special spindles or welding your own. Some dirt track racers use larger amounts of camber to try and find a fast way around the track.

The importance of the camber adjustment is to keep the maximum amount of tire tread on the ground during body roll. This is not as critical in karting as in stock cars. If you've been to your local Saturday night race track you may have noticed some of the extreme negative camber run on some right front tires. The intent is that in a corner, body roll will stand the tire straight up giving the tire a full contact patch in the corner when they most need it. Karts, because of their low center of gravity and rigid suspension, have no body roll.

On a kart the normal camber setting is zero when the wheels are pointed straight ahead. Because of the kingpin inclination when the kart is turned left the left front tire will develop positive camber and the right front will develop negative camber. This camber change causes weight transfer to the right front wheel so it becomes the dominating wheel.

TOE-IN

Toe-in is the effect of having the front edges of the tires closer together than the corresponding point at the rear edge of the tires. This effect tends to offset the tendency of the kart to wander.

As the kart hits irregularity in the track, the tire with the best traction will attempt to turn the kart slightly. This darting back and forth is called wander. This is compounded by any slop or wear in the steering components, and by the torque arm we discussed in the section on scrub radius. There is almost always some clearance in the kingpin and between the wheels and spindle stubs. The solution is to use some degree of toe-in. In karting it's not uncommon to run between zero and 1/8 of an inch toe-in. With the correct toe, the handling is more precise, with no trace of wander. The tires scrub less, run cooler and last longer.

WEIGHT DISTRIBUTION

Weight distribution is very important to the proper handling of a kart. It can be divided into two types. Static, which is when the kart is sitting still, and dynamic, which is what happens when the kart is in motion. When the kart is in motion any change in momentum or change of direction will cause a transfer of weight. Having some degree of control over the weight transfer is what makes for a well behaved kart.

Setting up the kart for proper weight distribution is covered under, "Initial Setup", but I will cover some of the reasons we do what we do here.

STATIC WEIGHT DISTRIBUTION

In almost all types of kart racing the chassis is setup with some amount of inside, or left side weight. Even on most road race type courses there are more left turns than right turns.

Unless you are competing in a class where you need to add a great deal of weight to meet class limits, you will soon find that driver placement is the single most important part of weight distribution. The driver should be placed as low as possible.

The weight distribution for sprint racing is usually set at 40/60 front to rear and 55/45 left to right. This is a good starting point. For oval track racing, dirt or pavement, the left to right ratio can change considerably. The recent introduction of LTO, (Left Turn Only), and offset chassis karts is a good indication of that.

The front weight bias should not drop below 40 percent. If the front is light, you will lose steering control, and the kart will understeer. This is especially true early in the race when the tires are cold. Another place were front weight is important is on cement tracks, such as found in indoor racing.

For dirt racing the answers are not quite so clear cut. In some of the unlimited and open classes which have a lot of horsepower available, you will want more rear weight to help get the power to the ground. It's not uncommon to pick the front end off the ground, even in some 4-cycle classes. The obvious problem with this is the lack of steering control. It is necessary to adjust your driving style to account for this. Full power can only be applied when the kart is pointed in the right direction. There is some doubt as to whether this type setup is really faster but it is rather common. Where horsepower is at a premium a more evenly balanced kart will work best.

DYNAMIC WEIGHT DISTRIBUTION

Dynamic weight distribution, or plain old weight transfer is what happens once the wheels start to roll. Just about everything effects the amount of weight transferred, and where it is being transferred too. We could go through a bunch of formulas and figure out exactly where every pound was going to go and when, but two things would probably happen. First, nobody would take the time to work through the numbers and second, when you got to the track the kart would probably be slower. I think we will just go through and tell you what seems to work best and take our best shot at why.

The biggest mass of weight to be considered is the driver. The driver pretty much determines the center of gravity of the kart. While the center of gravity is not commonly measured in karting it does still effect handling. The higher the center of gravity the more weight will be transferred. For the most part we want to keep the amount of weight transferred as low as possible. We want this mass as low as possible. The reason for this is that it represents a shift in the handling conditions of the kart. We need to drive the kart in a smooth fluid motion. You can't do that if you are constantly correcting for changes in handling characteristics all the way around the track.

When traveling in a straight line, whenever you step on the accelerator weight is transferred to the two rear tires in the same ratio as the left/right weight balance. When you deaccelerate weight is transferred to the front in the same ratio. Under these conditions the transfer is straight forward enough that the kart will tell us if something is amiss. If, when accelerating out of a mild corner, we find the front end becomes light and we lose steering control, it is a good indication that too much weight is being transferred to the rear wheels and it's necessary to add some front end weight. Under hard braking if too much weight is transferred forward, the rear will become skiddish, making the kart extremely hard to handle. Under hard braking we like all the weight in the rear.

Weight transfer during cornering is much

The front end of this kart is unique in the fact that it is a solid axle. The caster remains the same on both sides but is adjustable by rotating the axle.

more involved. Under normal conditions centrifugal force and the center of gravity cause weight to transfer to the outside front and rear corner of the kart. If you remember our discussion on spindles earlier you will remember that the kingpin inclination and caster angle on the wheel that is turning will also cause weight to be transferred. This is sometimes referred to as weight jacking although it is not the same method of weight jacking as used in stock car racing. The greater the caster angle on your frame the higher the jacking effect. Fig. 1 shows the stub axle with the steering straight, and the same stub axle with the steering turned to the left. Note how, if there is no wheel fitted the effect of the caster angle is to bring the tip of the stub axle nearer to the track surface. Of course with a tire fitted, the front of the frame is forced up or jacked. Most of this weight is transferred to the opposite rear corner. Transferring too much weight is a bad thing, so to offset some of that weight we do things like set static weight 55/45 left side/right side.

As we generally run 10 or 15 pounds more left side weight. Weight jacking for left and right turns is different. When we turn to the left the left front wheel may lift 70 pounds across the kart. But if we turn right we are asking the right front wheel to lift only 60 pounds, depending on the weight bias of the kart. So if we think of the frame as a torsion bar, the heavier wheel will not lift as high. Because of this weight jacking effect it's best not to get carried away with left side weight bias unless you are running an oval.

In road racing the 10 or 15 pounds of imbalance is hardly noticeable because most of the turns are left handers. If the weight balance is increased too much, this imbalance becomes unmanageable for road racing, but desirable for oval racing and we have what is called a LTO (Left Turn Only) kart or an offset chassis.

Another place where weight transfer is noticeable is if the track has a particularly bad bump. You may have noticed that if you cross the bump with the brakes on or the power off the bump seems more severe than when you cross it under some degree of acceleration. When you are under braking, the weight transferred is pushing the front of the kart down into the bump. If you cross it with mild acceleration, the front will be lifted over the bump. Do not become over aggressive on acceleration or you may cause rear wheel spin.

Another thing which effects dynamic weight distribution is frame stiffness or flex. Frame flex is quite a can of worms. In recent years almost all kart manufacturers have designed in various devices to adjust the flex in the frame. One method

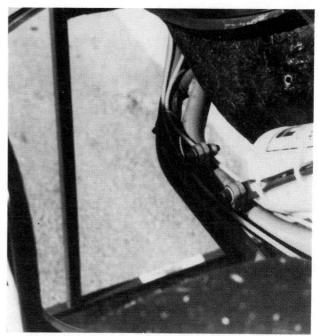

Another type of frame adjustment is to bolt two frame rails together for maximum stiffness or loosen the bolts for more flex.

is to cut one of the cross braces. The cut is left open for a loose condition. To tighten the chassis, a type of locking collar is mounted over the cut. Another manufacturer runs two side rails side by side near the seat. For a tight kart the rails are bolted together, for more flex the bolts are loosened or removed. Another type has an adjustable knob connecting the two rails together so the amount of flex can be adjusted during the race. At first appearance it looks like a weight jacker, while it is not a true weight jack it does control the frame stiffness, which effects how much weight is transferred.

There is a test called the "17 degree method", you can conduct to measure weight transfer when you are scaling your kart for static weight distribution. With the kart sitting on the scales and the driver in place, turn the steering wheel 17 degrees left or right and re-read the scale weight. You should find that the left front and the right rear gained about 8 to 10 percent more weight. If not the frame may be distorted or cracked.

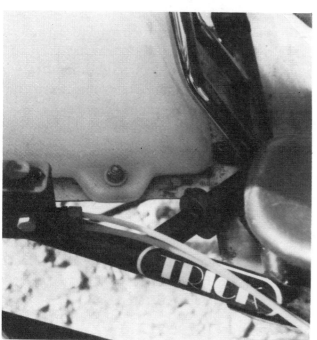

Frame stiffness is adjusted many ways. Trick karts use a short frame member on both sides of the seat which is split. To tighten the frame the split is bridged with a locking collar.

REAR AXLES

In kart racing we use what is called a live rear axle, or a locked rear end as it's called in stock car racing. This means both rear wheels turn together. While negotiating a turn, if both rear wheels are of similar size and have approximately the same weight, the inside wheel must scuff itself around the corner. This would lead to higher tire temperatures and excessive tire wear. If we transfer a little weight to the outside rear wheel, it will lighten the load on the inside wheel, and the scuffing action will be reduced.

We do this with dynamic weight transfer. Ideally we unload the wheel just enough to permit it to slip. As discussed in weight transfer above, when the left front raises, weight is transferred to the right rear, lightening the load on the left rear. This will permit enough tire slip to enable the kart to corner without loading down the engine. This is a fine line because as soon as the kart is straightened out on the straightaway you want the weight transferred back on both rear wheels. Maximum forward torque occurs when both tires are equally loaded.

Should you use an aluminum axle or a steel one? I have heard a lot of stories about aluminum axles flexing, and to some extent this may be true. I have had some experience with this on my sons kart. We could not keep a chain on it until we switched to a steel axle. But the problem may not have been entirely the fault of the aluminum axle.

On a kart with a lot of chassis flex the aluminum axle is subjected to a considerable amount of stress. Another thing that can add stress to the axle is if the kart has wide rear frame rail spacing. The aluminum axle works best with a stiff chassis or one which has three rear bearings. If you are having trouble keeping the chain on with an aluminum axle try tightening up the frame. If that doesn't help it's time to try a steel axle.

If your kart frame is rigid enough to handle it I would recommend you use the aluminum axle for all classes except maybe the open class. The lighter weight is a benefit because it's, rotational weight. The less rotational weight the quicker the kart should accelerate.

If you have a open class kart, with the motor driving the right side of the axle, with heavy loading on the left side it may be theoretically possible to twist the axle up like a torsion bar. Whether it really happens or not, I just don't know. I've heard the same argument for center mounted brake calipers, as opposed to those mounted on the left frame rail. However, I have seen no evidence of this happening. If your trying to transfer that much horsepower it's best to use a steel axle. I've driven both and I really don't think the average karter can notice the difference.

AXLE LENGTH

The length of the rear axle is best determined by track time and racing results, however a good starting point is generally somewhere in the 42" range. One trend in the last few years has been to use longer and longer rear axles. I feel that this is happening because the longer axles make it a little easier to setup the kart. I feel that this is not really fixing the karts handling problems. It's just a quick and easy way out of dailing in the chassis.

A long axle will make for more difficult racing in close quarters. It's more likely someone will run over your rear tire and get into your engine or worse yet, into you. The axle need be only long enough to make the kart handle properly. A general rule is the rear tires should be located only about three or four inches from the frame rail. An axle that provides you with a couple of inches of adjustment from that point should be sufficient.

A narrow rear track usually gives a kart lots of bite while a wide rear track will lead to a loose condition. The front and rear track should be near equal on a well behaved kart.

TIRE THEORY

This section covers tires in general. Things like air pressure, stagger and wheel spacing will be covered in the "Trackside" section, as they are used as a tuning aid in setting up your chassis. This section is more of an overview to give you information on tire construction and guide lines on how to get the most out of your tires.

NEW TIRES

If you want to go fast, your first trip should be to the tire store. There's no doubt about it, a kart will run faster on new tires. New tires can reduce lap times by as much as 1/2 second. There are few things you can do that will reduce your times as significantly as that. No matter how good you setup your kart, you can't replace the advantage of new rubber.

Ideally, you should run new tires every time you race, however few of us are in a financial position to do this. There are karters out there that run new tires each week. Theres always someone who will spend whatever it takes to win. I know others that buy a new set one week, soften them for the next two weeks and repeat the cycle throughout the season. I also know karters that never buy a new tire, and for the most part they are running in the middle of the pack. How good do you want to run? It's a question only you can answer. It boils down to how often can you afford to buy new tires?

The biggest drawback with new tires is, they aren't new very long. Hopefully the other competitors in your class can't afford new tires every week either. Depending on how often you race and how much practicing you do, you should be able to run 4 or 5 race days. As the tires age, your lap times will creep up. The change is usually so gradual, you may not notice it. Then all of a sudden you realize that your losing ground. If you are running for a point title, you may be forced to buy new rubber every week. If you are just trying to do the best you can without spending a lot of money, I would recommend you start each new season with a new set of rubber. If at mid-season you are running pretty good but find that you are starting to lose a few ticks on the old stop watch you may want to buy another set.

Improving the handling of our kart does not end with buying a new set of tires. You may have just gained 1 / 2 second and be tickled pink, but I suspect we can find a few more tenths in there if we work at it. First lets talk about the tires themselves. Then we'll go into making them work with your chassis.

BRAND NAMES

The brand of tires you run is not the important issue. If you walk through the pits and talk to several of the drivers you will find all brands and a million reasons why each driver prefers a particular brand. In the highly competitive kart market we enjoy today, all the major tire companies are producing a wide range of sizes and compounds.

I think it's safe to say that you can make a chassis handle with any brand if you take the time to work with it. For a newcomer the only good answer is check out what the other competitors in the class you will be running are using and start there. If you stick with a major brand and a relatively soft compound, you won't be too far off. Some clubs have gone to a club tire which is usually a harder compound to keep cost down. This tire is currently the Burris M15B. The idea of a club tire is good because you can generally run all year on one set of tires. Some tracks have only one or two classes which run the club tire.

TIRE BREAK IN

All the manufacturers I spoke with recommend new tires be run in. They indicated it was very important. The accepted procedure is to run the tires the day before a race for 10 to 12 laps, pushing them just enough to get them up to operating temperature. They should then be allowed to cool completely. Stone cold, as one representative stated it. Overnight should be sufficient. This will allow the rubber to cure correctly. Proper curing is important for longer life.

TIRE COMPOUNDS

The selection of which tire compound to use is complicated by the fact that there is no universal system between manufacturers. You will have to determine which tire works the best for you through trial and error. Every kart and every driver is different, and it seems like the manufacturers are always changing the compounds. I suppose it's all for product improvement but is sure keeps things confusing. I can not tell you which tire compound to use, but I can give you some basic facts which may help you make that decision.

Kart tires come in so many brands, types, and compounds it's hard to know which to run.

16

It's generally easier to set up a kart with softer tires. Being soft they give the driver more feeling of control. You need to use a little care here. If you set up your kart with soft tires and then allow them to get old and hard, or switch to a harder compound, your handling may go away. A setup with soft tires will require replacing tires more often as soft tires wear faster. This translates into more dollars. That is the main reason some tracks have gone to running a class or two with a club tire, which is generally a hard compound tire. Tires do change as they wear, they get harder not softer. Your lap times will slowly increase as the season progresses, and the tire hardens. If you are in a tight point race, your only hope of keeping your lap times down is a new set of rubber every third or fourth race day. It's not uncommon for some drivers to run new rubber each race day. Who said racing was cheap?

The sun is perhaps the most damaging thing to a set of tires. Spares and unused tires should be stored out of the sunlight. You shouldn't leave them lay out exposed in the back of a pick up truck.

TIRE SIZE

Tires now come in two wheel diameters. The more common 5 inch rims, and the newer 6 inch rims. Which one you run is really not a concern for this book, as you can set up your kart to win with either. Actually there is very little difference between the two. The 6 inch rims have a lower profile tire, which means less sidewall flex but the ride height of the kart ends up about the same.

I have heard that in long races 5" tires tend to lose speed, while a 6" tire will gain or stay even. I don't know if this is true or not, as I have not run 6" tires, but I can't see any basis for this, other than the fact the stiffer sidewall would cause less flexing, which would create less heat, allowing the tire to run a bit cooler. I have seen some karters running a combination of 6" on the rears and 5" on the front. Here again the smaller side wall on the rear may give the kart more stability in a long race. The disadvantage is it's necessary to purchase another set of rims. This is no small expense.

TIRE WIDTH

Tire width on the rear is a decision which is generally based on available horsepower. One rule of thumb is, the more horsepower available, the wider the tire you can use. A wider tire gives a bigger contact patch which translates to better traction, and more horsepower to the ground, however, you must realize the bigger the tire, the more horsepower it is going to take to get it rolling. If you are racing a restricted or stock 4-cycle class, you must understand that there is not an abundance of horsepower available. You only want a tire wide enough to do the job. A stock Briggs can not pull a 7 inch rear tire. For a stock Briggs a 5.5 or 6.00 rear is the norm. Modifieds and opens can run 7.00 and 7.50's. A 100cc 2-cycle can also pull a 7.00 nicely.

Tire width on the front is somewhat different than for the rear. In this case the smaller the better. All you really need in a front tire, is a tire that will give you sufficient bite in the corners. Remember that the added weight and drag of a larger tire will affect what power you have to push the kart around the track. The 4.50 has become the norm, except in dirt racing, where it's not uncommon to run a larger right front.

Tire width is not only determined by the tires size, but is also affected by the width of the rims they are mounted on. Choosing the correct rim size will depend on two things, sidewall flex, and the amount of offset you want. Sidewall flex is not a major, or at least should not be a major concern. Sidewall flex should only occur if you are running unusually low tire pressures or have a excessive amount of weight transfer. As a rule a rim width about equal to the width of the tire tread will give a reasonable amount of sidewall flex, where a rim width larger than the tread width will give less flex. Most of the time you will find a rim from 1/4 to 1/2 inch wider than the tread width will work best. This allows the contact patch to set flat to the track. Wider rim allow the tread to be spread to the corners of the tire causing the center to bow in. This will cause a loss of contact with the track, unless larger air pressure is used. Narrower rim widths tend to round the contact patch giving less contact area. It's about the same thing as running the next size smaller tire. Using a slightly smaller rim width will also tend to make a tire slightly taller. This is sometimes used on front tires to increase ride height and change stagger.

WHEEL RIMS

The decision to be made on rims is whether to use single piece rims or two piece rims. Should you have single piece rims, your adjustments may be more limited. Because of the price of single piece rims you will probably have only a few sizes to choose from. Using two piece rims allows you a countless number of combinations, and you can usually pick up used wheel halves at a swap meet at a reasonable price. This usually means you will have more flexibility in selecting tire widths and stagger combinations. A large selection of mounted tires is perhaps more important to the dirt track racer than the pavement driver, but it's nice to have the option available.

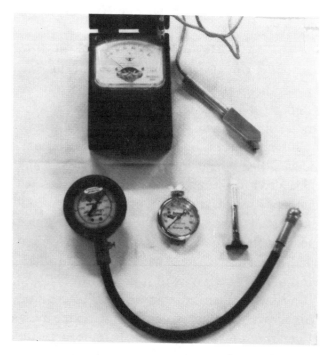

Some of the tools used to check tires. A tire Pyrometer for testing temperature, air pressure gauge, Durometer for testing hardness, and a Tread Depth gauge.

DUROMETERS

The hardness of a tire can be measured using a durometer. If you have such a meter, when you buy a new set of tires you should measure the hardness of the rubber and record this information for future use. As the season goes along, you can compare this reading with the present reading. You will find the reading getting higher, indicating that the tire is becoming harder. This happens because the tire heats up when running and cools down between races. This cycling causes the rubber to cure and harden.

There is some black magic in reading tires. It's not fair to read them one day in 90 degree sunshine and compare that to a reading taken after spending a week in a cold dark garage. Always try to keep the measuring conditions the same. As a rule, I only use this information to insure that I don't accidentally end up with 3 soft tires mated up with a hard one. However, in dirt racing this is sometimes desirable.

The hardness of a tire is controlled by the compound of which it is made. A new tire might have a durometer reading of 48. A soft tire, such as a Bridgestone YEM should read around 42 while a harder tire, such as a Burris M15 will read about 52. Over the years tires have been getting softer. As in NASCAR and Indy car racing, soft tires go faster, and everybody likes to go fast. It's also good advertising for the tire companies. The only problem for us is they also wear out faster.

PYROMETER

Another testing aid for tires is a pyrometer. A pyrometer measures tire temperature. The tire manufacturers and big buck teams use infrared meters, which read the temperature across the tire in a matter of seconds. The rest of us use a contact type, which requires a bit more time. A pyrometer can tell you if your setup is correct at trackside. Let's say you come in off the track and your left rear tire is reading hotter than your right rear tire. This

18

indicates the left tire is carrying more load than the right. It might indicate that your tire air pressures are off or even that the weight distribution is off. Tire temperatures should be read in three places across the tire. The inside, outside and middle. Higher temperatures on both outside and inside compared to the middle might indicate that your air pressure is too low for that tire. Higher temperature in the middle would tell you the tire air pressure is too high, and higher temperatures on only one side is probably trying to indicate the caster, camber or tire position is incorrect. Tire temperature variances from tire to tire indicates incorrect weight distribution. If you are working with a kart with adjustable camber, tire temperature can help you sort out the correct setup. If the inside edge of the tire is always hot, it is an indication that you have too much negative camber.

Unless you have one of the inferred temperature meters or a pit crew member who can jump on the kart as soon as the race is over, I would not recommend you try using a pyrometer on race day. Best results are obtained on practice days when you can stop right away and measure the tires. On a race day you usually have a cool down lap and have to spend time going across the scales. It is almost impossible to get a good consistent reading after all this. Tire temperature from session to session is not the important issue. Temperature from tire to tire and across each tire is the information you are after.

If you don't have a pyrometer you can still tell a little about tire temperature by visually examining the tires after a race. If the surface of the tire appears smooth and shiny the tire is probably running a little cool. If the tire has a build up of rubber on it's surface the, tire is running hot. The tire should have a dull fine textured look to it. Something like the appearance of a sheet of fine emery cloth.

If the tire has rubber build up on it from running hot, should it be removed? Quite often you will see a pit member with a heat gun and a scraper cleaning the excess rubber off. I would have to say that this is the preferred thing to do. You don't know for sure if the build up is only your own tire rubber, or if it's a composite of rubber laying on the track, but it's a good bet it's not layered uniformly around the tire, so it's best to remove it. Another

school of thought is to ignore it as it will usually wear off quickly as the tires heat to operating temperature. The only problem with this is your handling may be a bit inconsistent for the first couple of laps, which tend to be the most important.

Don't worry so much about removing the build up that you forget to cure the cause of the problem. An attempt should be made to unload the tire to reduce its operating temperature.

TIRE BALANCING

You may feel that balancing kart tires is a waste of time, however, I feel you should start every race with everything the very best you can make it and hope things stay that way for as long as possible. Balancing may not help, but it sure won't hurt. The faster the racing speed, the more important balancing becomes.

There are two types of balancing. Static balancing, which is the type where you use a bubble balancer, and Dynamic balancing, which is a spin type balancer. The most common form used in karting is to spin the tire and wheel assembly by hand on a short piece of axle.

Most commercial spin balancers cannot handle a tire the size of our kart tires. However, if you have a friend who has a balancer and will work with you, it can be done. It is necessary to remove a high percentage of the weight from the balancer so it can detect the smaller out of balance of the smaller tire. If you remove the automotive mounting adapters and install a rear axle hub directly on the balancer, it will do a pretty good job.

Balancing the rear tires is not quite as important as balancing the fronts because of the live axle used in karting. However I feel some effort in this area is time well spent.

The thing that most often causes an out of balance tire is generally not the tire itself, but the wheel it is mounted on. The biggest culprit in this respect is the valve stem. Another problem is using different size nuts, missing nuts, and or a mixture of washers used to assemble the wheel halves. Don't overlook the possibility of a bent rear axle. This will be discused later.

Some karters advocate balancing the individual wheel halves and tire separately. While that is good, I just don't have time for that. I don't know about you, but for me there never seems to be enough time to do all the things I would like to do. I prefer to put it all together and balance the whole thing at one time. Yes, it might take 1/2 oz. or so more weight to balance the wheel but it is about ten times faster.

If you wish to balance each piece, the following procedure will help you do it.

It is not necessary to balance individual wheel halves. Bolt two halves together and spin them as an assembly. If you are using two halves which each have a valve stem, mount them opposite to each other to offset the weight. If you are using new rims without valve stems, this procedure will help you locate where to drill the valve stem hole. Do not attempt to balance the wheels on the kart. Mount your fixture in a vise so the only thing rotating is the wheel to be balanced. Spin the rim and mark the bottom of the rim when it stops spinning. If the wheel is out of balance, after several spinnings the marks you made will start showing up in one area. This area will be the heaviest portion of the wheel. You should drill the valve stem hole opposite the heavy side. The valve stem will offset the heavy side. Locate the valve stem hole between a pair of mounting holes. This will allow easy access to the hub bolts without

interference from the valve stem. Do not recess the stem too deep into the rim, or you will be unable to put air in the tire when it is mounted on the kart without removing the wheels. Some karters like to mount the stem in the inside wheel half to avoid the possibility of a competitor getting into the wheel and tearing the stem out. I have found that this makes it very difficult to adjust air pressures at the track. I prefer the stem in the outside rim. If you use very short valve stems you shouldn't have a problem. In 20 years of racing, I think I have only seen one valve stem ripped out by a competitor.

After installing the valve stem, spin the wheel again. This time mark the inner half of the rim at the bottom when it stops it's rotation. Spin the wheel several more times, marking the wheel each time. If the marks should fall into a certain area, it means that the entire wheel assembly is heavier at that point. To try and make the rim assembly roll true you can try turning the inner rim one bolt at a time and spin test after each adjustment, or you can add wheel weight. If after several spins the marks are scattered all over the rim it's a good indication that the wheel is balanced. Mark the rims with a punch mark for future alignment reference.

Install the rubber "O" ring, or sealing plate, and the tire on the rim, but do not seat the bead. Instead give yourself the ability to rotate the tire should you need to. Now spin the the whole assembly again several times, marking the bottom

When balancing tires it is best to use a couple of small weights instead of one large one. Added weights should be secured with RTV.

each time. Should you find the marks end up in one location again, rotate the tire on the rim and spin test again. Through this rotation of the tire on the rim you may eventually get to a point where the heaviest portion of the tire will match up with the lightest portion of the rim and your tire/wheel balance will be correct. If the tire assembly still ends up with the marks all in one area it will be necessary to add weight. You can purchase self sticking weight from an automotive store. The weight should be added opposite the heavy end, or marks. If the amount of weight to be added is considerable, you should add two smaller weights and spread them out. After you are satisfied with the balance job you should secure the weights to the wheels with RTV or similar adhesive.

As you can see this is a very involved and time consuming procedure. If time is a premium for you, as it is for most of us, you can balance the whole assembly and add the necessary weight. The degree of accuracy required depends on the type and speed of classes you are participating in. Obviously, Enduro karts require balanced tires while 1/10 mile dust bowls do not.

In dirt racing the wheel can pick up a lot of mud and clumps of dirt from the track. The wheels should be cleaned after each race.

OLD TIRES

How do you know when the tires are getting hard? As the tires get harder, they tend to slip more (lose bite), especially when cold. When the tires are cold the rear will be loose and the front will have a great deal of understeer. As the tires reach proper operating temperature, the handling returns to normal. The older and harder the tires become the more time required for them to reach operating temperature. At first you may notice it only takes one or two laps to get the tires up to operating temperature. 3 or 4 weeks later you may notice that it takes 4 or 5 laps to get the tires up to snuff. When this happens it's time for a trip to the tire store. If bucks are tight, you may be able to postpone this for a couple of weeks by using one of the commercially available softeners, the only answer is new tires.

A case of severe tire damage. It makes the kart very difficult to handle. This particular tire was a recap. Recaps should be inspected regularly for tread seperation.

TIRE SOFTENERS

With many tracks specifying hard tire classes, many karters are looking for a way to soften up those old hard bricks. Softeners or conditioners can help somewhat but are illegal at some tracks. However, in most cases it is not illegal to soften the tires at home. Tire softeners and conditioners attempt to compensate for the aging effects of the tire compound.

How well do softeners work? That is a very difficult question to answer. I have found that the softeners effect usually wears off after a couple of laps. However, the first couple of laps are perhaps the most important of the race. I usually avoid its use unless I'm trying to get one or two more races out of an old set of tires, such as at the end of the season. I suspect in the long run, you're money and time ahead to just buy new rubber a couple of times a year.

If you are going to use a softener you should stick with the commercially available softeners, other chemicals such as Toluene & Xylene are dangerous. These solvents can get into your body by breathing them in from the air or through the skin. They can hurt you, so it is best to avoid them. Use something you know is safe.

RAIN TIRES

In karting the distinction between rain and dirt tires is not really clear, but there is a noticeable difference if you know what you are looking for. Not all manufacturers build true rain tires. A true rain tire will have definite channels for the water to flow through. The tread pattern will have a couple of full depth circumferential grooves to receive the water from the contact patch and also a series of swept back lateral grooves or bends which usually lead to the outside edges. True dirt tires usually have a lot of square and rectangular shaped blocks interlaced. Similar to looking at a brick wall. Currently, several tires are marketed as rain/dirt. While rain tires will work reasonably well on dirt, dirt tires don't work so good in rain.

With the increasing growth and publicity of karting, I think we will see more true rain tires on the market in the future. Rain tires are usually of a soft compound. A soft compound is necessary because the water running through the channels cool the rubber. The soft compound combined with the smaller foot print carrying the weight of the kart, generates heat causing the tires to wear rapidly on a dry track. If you are caught on a drying

You can tell this is a rain tire because it has circumferential grooves to channel the water and curved grooves to dispel the water. Rain tires must be mounted for the proper rotation. This tire would be coming toward you.

track with rain tires, you should steer for the wet patches, and hope the race is over soon or you're in for another trip to the tire store.

Rain tires must be mounted in the correct direction if they are to channel the water out from under the tire. The center of tread pattern should make contact with the track first.

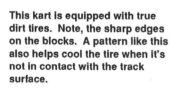

This kart is equipped with true dirt tires. Note, the sharp edges on the blocks. A pattern like this also helps cool the tire when it's not in contact with the track surface.

This tire is often used for dirt or rain. In this case the compound is the important thing to know. A true rain tire is usually of a soft compound. The deep circumferential grooves are good for water. The blocks have rounded edges but they are not aligned as you would expect for a rain tire. The holes in the center of the blocks are to help dissipate heat but are more often found on dirt tires. I suspect the Vega tire engineers know a lot more about tires than I do.

DIRT TIRES

A lot of the success of racing on dirt has to do with tire selection. A racer must not only choose the brand of the tire he wishes to run, but also must choose from a number of compounds and tread designs. Tire decisions made in the pits greatly affect the karts handling, and in fact may be the most important decision made on race day. This decision can often win or lose a race. Unfortunately, the manufacturers do not give us a lot to choose from in the area of tread design. For this reason it's not uncommon to see several do-it-yourself tread patterns.

The average karter makes his decision by seeing what tire is used most often at the track he is planning to run. Then he asks the neighboring pit crew what tire pressure they are running and duplicates his neighbors set up. This may be a good way to start the first practice session, but it will not put you up front in the feature.

Some tread patterns work better on hard dry tracks while others are better on tacky tracks. Soft tacky tracks need a tire with a shallow tread pattern while hard tracks need something like a soft slick that grip or adhere to the surface. Most dirt track drivers have at least two different tire compounds and several stagger combinations with them when they show up for a race.

There's also the fact that the dirt track surface changes from race to race and throughout the night. To compensate for this change some racers change the tread patterns, mixing different brand tires or by making their own tread pattern. This is called grooving or siping.

Grooving is the removal of rubber from a tire in such a way as to cause grooves to be made, similar to the grooves that exist between blocks or ribs on tires. Siping means the placement of a razor cut or slit in the surface of a tire which does not cause the removal of any rubber.

One advantage of grooving and siping is that it tends to make a hard tire bite as if it were a softer tire.

Putting in grooves or sipes circumferentially around a tire will aid in steering, while grooves or sipes that run across the face of a tire will aid in bite and braking. When working with a treaded tire follow the block pattern already on the tire. Groove or sipe each block down its middle for the desired effect. On slicks you can pretty much design your own tread pattern.

Care must be exercised so as not to groove or sipe too deep or you may cut into the cord of the carcass. The actual rubber depth on kart tires in only about 5/32. When you get out to the edges of the tread it really thins out.

Grooving requires a lot of elbow grease. Heated grooving irons have been developed that slice the groove out a bit easier. Siping knives are simply handles that have very thin razor style blades at their ends. It helps to sprinkle talcum powder on the tire before you begin. A really soft tire is more difficult to cut because the rubber tends to grab at the knife as you try to cut it.

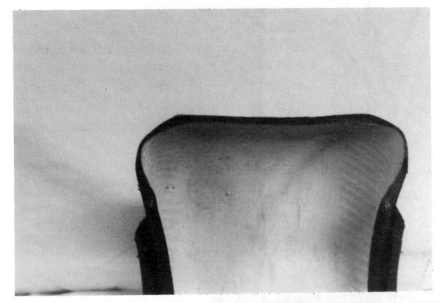

Ever wonder how much tread there was between you and the road. Note how thin the side wall is. Maybe we should take those corners a little easier.

Most kart tires have wear indicators molded into the surface. The indicators not only tell you how much rubber is left, they can be used to gage the camber setting of the kart. They should wear evenly across the tire.

AERODYNAMICS

This chapter is not intended to make you an Aeronautical Engineer. It's purpose is to make you aware of some of the aeronautical principles which may apply to karting.

Does aerodynamics have a place in karting? Do we go fast enough in karts to justify an aerodynamic effort? The answer to these questions is yes to some extent. If you don't think aerodynamics is a factor at our lower speeds drive down the road in a car at 30 miles an hour and stick your hand out the window. There is quite a force exerted on your hand. Your hand only presents 18 square inches of frontal area to the wind stream. A person sitting in a kart presents approximately 5 square feet of frontal area to the wind stream. That's a significant amount. When most of us think of aerodynamics, we think of wings and tunnels such as used in NASCAR and Indy car racing. While these aerodynamics principles hardly apply to sprint karts, there is one aspect of aerodynamics which is prevalent in karts, and that is drag.

In karting we need to direct our efforts to reducing drag. This is best done by reducing the air penetration quality of a chassis. By streamlining the kart, we lower drag coefficients thereby increasing acceleration and straightaway speeds.

DRAG

Drag can be identified as any kind of resistance to the forward motion of the kart. There are three types of drag. There is form drag, friction drag and induced drag. Form drag is the drag caused by the turbulence which is present in the area immediately following the kart. Friction drag is the drag caused by air friction as the air moves in and around all the protrusions on the kart. Induced drag is drag which is created for a beneficial purpose such as to create down force. We will discuss how all of these effect us as karters.

FORM DRAG

Form drag has become more well known because of its effect in NASCAR racing. Because of form drag, we have slipstreams and slingshots.

Form drag arises because the airflow over and around a vehicle does not close in completely around the rear of the vehicle but separates to form a wake. The wake leaves a pocket of stable low pressure air up close to the rear of the vehicle. The size of the pocket can be controlled by the shape of the body passing through the air. The pocket also intensifies as velocity or speed increases. In racing, we can take advantage of form drag by pulling up directly behind a competitor into the pocket of stable air. This allows us to travel just as fast as the leading vehicle without using as much power. Driving in the pocket is called drafting. An interesting note is that while drafting helps the competitor following, by lessening his air resistance, it also benefits the leading competitor as long as the follower remains behind in the slipstream. The result is both competitors go faster. This is due to more favorable air flow wake dissipation, and characteristics associated with prolonging the wake turbulence. Racing in the pocket, or slipstream as it's sometimes called, also opens up the possibility of a slingshot around the leading vehicle. The reason for this is two fold. First you can pick up just a little bit of momentum before you swing out and break the slipstream, or wake, and second when the wake is broken it will fill back in behind the lead vehicle slowing it slightly.

The effects of form drag in karting is more noticeable in Enduro and faster forms of sprint racing, such as banked ovals, street racing and the very fast shifter classes. Form drag, though used for slipstreaming or slingshot moves, is a bad thing and should be reduced. The reason it is bad is it reduces the forward speed of the kart, and you don't particularly want a competitor on your rear bumper, where he can slingshot pass you. If form drag is reduced, the pocket will be so small the trailing kart can not fit into it and it will have no advantage.

Reducing form drag in karting is not as easy as in full body stock cars. The automobile industry learned several years ago that if they chopped off the rear of a car straight up and down both at the rear window and at the rear deck, gas mileage went up. The reason was a reduction in form drag. In karts it is difficult to chop off the rear nice and clean. The

only recourse we have is to keep things like exhaust pipes, catch cans and number panels up tight, close to the back of the seat or down as low as possible so the air can drop in behind the driver as soon as possible.

FRICTION DRAG

Friction drag is perhaps the most prevalent in sprint kart racing. It is generated by air sticking to the surface of a body and forming a boundary layer because of air viscosity. Due to the nature of a karts structure it is an inherently dirty vehicle aerodynamically and presents many problems in reducing friction drag. Friction drag can be reduced, but never eliminated, by use of body panels, nose cones and front scoops. The panels surface should be very smooth. It's a good idea to keep the body panels clean and waxed.

The best way to reduce friction drag is by streamlining the kart as much as possible. The term streamlined, when applied correctly, means that a body is carefully shaped so as to leave behind only a small wake. In other words, the design emphasis is carried out to produce as little form drag as possible. Looking at a kart chassis we can clearly see that it would be impossible to close up all the

The aerodynamics on this kart are very good. Good enough to be a track champion.

open areas. The best you can do is reduce frontal area where possible, get legs and arms tucked in and keep the airflow between front and rear wheels moving as undisturbed and smoothly as possible. This is why it is wise to produce rounded surfaces, particularly those in leading edge capacities.

In the last year or so we have seen karters extending their floor pan rearward below the seat and engine area. This should improve air flow, but at this point in time I don't know if it's something everyone should do.

A full floor pan should improve air flow. How beneficial they are in karting is still to be determined.

INDUCED DRAG

Induced drag is a product of wings and spoilers, which have little importance to the average karter. If you race in a class that allows these things, they will be covered at the end of this chapter.

TESTING FOR DRAG

We know that drag plays a key role in the speed and performance of any kart. Here is a cheap and dirty way to measure drag. You will need a length of flat track, a school parking lot will do. Mark two spots on your course or use two prominent objects

as your starting and ending points. They should be a minimum of a couple hundred feet apart. Then bring your kart up to a moderate speed, say 5000 rpm. As you reach your start point start the stopwatch and take your foot off the accelerator, letting the kart coast. When you reach the second mark, stop the stopwatch and record the time. This will be your baseline for any further test. If your time increases, you are going slower and the modifications hurt your speed. If the time decreases, whatever you did made the kart move through the air more easily or roll more freely, and helped your speed. The test should be done in both directions to cancel out any variations caused by a slight incline in the track or wind condition that may be present. Add your times together and divide by two in order to get the average. If you run tests during wide temperature ranges the results may not be as accurate. If the temperature is 110 and sunny, the air will be thin and easy to pass through. If a later test is done at 64, the air will be heavier and harder to push through. Humidity will make a big difference also. It is always best to run a baseline test each day just to insure you know where you are starting from.

A benifical use of a number panel but I suspect if he as to change gears to many times the panel will disappear.

These panels are of questionable value. Any pressure exerted on them during cornering would simply bend them. Cosmetically they are nice.

IMPROVING DRAG

It is easy to understand that any reduction in drag pays dividends in speed and is well worth the effort. The easiest way to reduce air drag is through frontal area reduction. This primarily means that the kart and driver should punch a smaller hole through the air. In this area, number panel placement can become very critical. The front panel should not be mounted straight up and down on the front bumper. The panel should be inclined or mounted on a fairing in front of the steering wheel. Some karters mount their front panel up front and punch a series of holes in the panel to allow air flow. If the holes are 1/2 inch or smaller, they offer little reduction in frontal area. Side panels should be inclined to insure the air flow flows out and around the kart.

The engine is an important consideration. It's situation is the opposite because the engine relies on air flow for cooling. For a 2-cycle engine, all it's cooling is from air flow. Caution must be observed so as not to block a direct flow of clean fresh air from flowing across the head and upper cylinder. For a 4-cycle engine, the cooling air flow is some what different, as the flywheel fins act as an air pump forcing air around the cylinders and across the head. However, caution must be exercised so as not to block the shroud on the outside of the engine. Some shroud covers sold today greatly

restrict the air flow. The placement of body side pods and number panels must not interfere with the passage of clean air.

Reductions in rolling resistance will also help to increase speed but not to the same degree as drag reduction. Most of the help in this area comes from using low friction bearings. Axles should spin freely with no binding. If you are running tracks with long straights or a lot of straights, you need to keep things like toe-in, camber, and stagger as neutral as possible. Most of the front edges should be well rounded and smooth. The overall shape should be somewhat flat, with only gradual

The type of driver fairing is not important. It is best to use one of some type.

changes in body contour. The bottom should be flat and as uncluttered as possible. The rear, on the other hand, should be square and sharp, not rounded at all.

Air has a natural tendency to stick to adjacent particles of air. When it gets separated, such as when your kart slices through it, it wants to come back together again at the back of the kart. This can most easily be accomplished by having a sharp, square shape at the rear. This does not seem like it should be so, but wind tunnel testing by Detroit auto makers does show that a rounded shape tends to promote turbulence as the air exits the rear of a vehicle, which increases both drag and lift.

FAIRINGS AND SPOILERS

Fairings and spoilers are pretty much the same thing in kart racing. They are devices which spoil or otherwise alter natural air flow around the kart. Their primary purpose in karting is to smooth air flow over the chassis. Sprint karts are very dirty aerodynamically. There are far to many open areas and pockets to trap air. Anything we can do to smooth the flow of air over the kart will reduce drag and therefore increase lap times. The important thing to remember is to avoid sharp leading edges, surface irregularities and high drag profiles or pockets. The karts profile should be designed so as to produce the smallest surface area and a smooth constant air flow. Air should not be permitted to stagnate or pile up on any portion of the spoiler or fairing.

One question that has always bothered me was just how effective fairings are in karting. I decided to conduct a little experiment. I made a platform and mounted a silhouette of a man sitting in the kart. We rigged it with pullys, wires and a scale so we could measure the loading applied to the silhouette. This silhouette became known as Speedy. Well, my son and I must have pulled old Speedy up and down the road about a hundred times. It may have not been very scientific but we learned some very interesting things. First we drove up and down

the road at various speeds just to see what kind of numbers we would get. The test showed that from 35 to 60 miles per hour the wind loading was linear with speed. For every five mph. increase in speed there was an approximately 2 pound increase in loading on the silhouette. We then mounted a Top Line Short Hood fairing, and repeated the test. The results were a bit surprising, below 50 mph. the wind loading was only reduced by 1/2, (50 percent). At 55 and 60 mph. the loading was reduced by 1/3, (33 percent). This may have been caused by interference from the tow vehicle, but as it wasn't evident in the no fairing test, I'm not sure. The outcome is still the same, the fairing did reduce wind loading by 1/2 even at the relatively slow speed of 30 mph.

We next tried a more modern Stallion sprint fairing. This was a real surprise. The improvement below 50 mph. was only 1/3 (33 percent), and above 50 mph. was only 20 percent. Even through the Stallion flaring had more surface area it reduced the wind loading less. The only reason I can think of to account for this is that the CKS fairing was slightly longer and about one inch wider on each side, this caused the Top Line fairing to mount about one inch higher above the steering wheel.

Keep in mind that this was not a controlled test. My purpose was not to test individual fairings, but to prove if any fairing was a benefit. I think I have proved that a fairing can reduce wind load by as much as 50 percent. This is a significant reduction in drag. For a 4-cycle engine, this can mean a considerable increase in horsepower delivered to the road. For a 2-cycle, the increase may not be as noticeable, but it is still an increase. This experiment shows that some type of spoiler should be mounted in front of the driver. Just think of what we could do if we had a wind tunnel!

On high speed tracks, some provision for forward wheel fairings is also a good idea since wheels and tires are responsible for a fair amount of drag and wake turbulence. Some organizations now prohibit nose cones and wheel fairings which extend in front of the front bumper. Check with your local track before installing these items on your kart.

This type fairing is prehaps better than it first appears. It will deflect the air around the driver. It is just tall enough to flow air up and over the drivers helmet. You will also note cooling air to the motor is unobstructed. The front number panel would work better if it were inclined a bit.

INDUCED DRAG

I am not sure how beneficial this section will be to your current racing plans, but perhaps it will give you something to think about.

Induced drag is a function of using wings and air foils. A wing added to a sprint kart may look nice but it is of questionable value. It would take a long track and high speeds before any real benefit would be realized.

Currently, wings as we see them in sprint car racing, are not allowed in kart racing. I personally think this is a good thing but I suspect someday in the future they will be allowed in some form or other. I have seen some effort to turn the front fairing into a wing and attempts to spread a wing across the rear tires. It is very difficult to make these methods beneficial, because it is almost impossible to get clean air to the wing. The wing really needs to be up in the free air, such as at the top of the cage on a cage kart.

There are karts which could benefit from wings. Speedway karts are one, Shifters and Enduros are a couple of others. One thing that is often not considered is that it takes some amount of horsepower to push a wing through the air. A wing is not a perpetual motion machine. In order to

achieve down force a wing must be propelled through the air. To obtain satisfactory results the horsepower must be available to do the job. For this reason, you will find the benefits of a wing greater on a 2-cycle than on a 4-cycle.

Getting into the study of wings and airfoils can get pretty involved. If you really want to get serious, a trip to your local library may be in order. There are several good books written on wings. I will only include some basic principles here.

The two principal characteristics of a wing that are a concern to us is lift, which when turned upside down translates into down force, and drag.

Lift results from air flow and the resultant pressure differential across a wing. The air flowing across the longer upper surface must increase in velocity to join like air flow traveling across the lower surface. The increase in velocity yields a decrease in pressure to produce an upward lifting component. Since we are not interested in lift but instead downward pressure, we simply turn the wing upside down.

Another important aspect of using a wing is its angle of attack. The more angle the wing is given the more downward pressure is exerted on the rear tires, giving you lots of bite. The down side of this is the dreaded induced drag. The increased angle of the wing causes drag when shooting down the straight-a-ways.

Adjusting a wing is always a trade off between more bite in the turns versus more straight-a-way speed. The more horsepower and the smaller the track, the more angle of attack you can use. For a stock Briggs engine on a small track the wing would need to be nearly flat. Being nearly flat minimizes the benefits of more bite in the corners.

There are ways to enhance a wings effectiveness. One method is to install wing tip end plates. These plates increase the effective aerodynamic aspect ratio by changing the airflow over the wing. The end plates required can be quite large but can reduce drag by as much as 40% at all speeds. It will reduce drag but not eliminate it. If you've watched any winged sprint cars, I'm sure you've seen that the wing tips are as big as the wing itself. If you are going to experiment with wings you should by all means use wing tips.

Wing placement is just as important as the wing itself. The wing must be able to receive good clean air if it is to be effective. A wing mounted low, and hidden behind a driver and a motor would be of questionable value.

One good way to produce down force at the tire contact patch while running small angles of attack, (thereby achieving lower drag) is to mount the wing as far away from the axle centerline as possible. As far forward for front wings and as far rear ward for rear wings. This mounting produces greater down force on the respective tire contact patches than it would if mounted directly above the axles.

The surface finish on a wing is critical, especially the front one third of the wing. The idea is to eliminate flow separation with a smooth surface. As the wing gets sandblasted use fine sandpaper to smooth it out. Dents, holes and protrusions in the wing surface top or bottom can also cause flow separation. Fill dents and holes and remove protrusions for best efficiency.

The lower surface flow on the wing is just as important as the top surface. Wing mounts under the wing mess up the flow, especially where the mounts are in the wing. Keep access holes to a minimum size, cover them when possible and streamline the mounts as much as possible.

When working with wings there are a few terms you should be familiar with: Angle of attack, stall, tip plates, flaps and aerodynamic balance. We will briefly cover them here.

What is the *Angle of attack*? The angle of attack is the angle from horizontal that a wing is set at. Increasing the angle of attack will increase the down force developed by the wing. It will also increase the amount of drag up to the point that the wing stalls (all drag, no down force), becomes ineffective. The most efficient angle of attack is usually between 6 and 12 degrees. The most beneficial angle of attack depends on a compromise between down force in the corners, drag down the straightaway and the horsepower available.

Stall. Stall is the point where the angle of attack is great enough to cause the air flow to separate from the wing surface. This causes turbuleoint where the angle of attack is great enough to cause the air flow to separate from the wing surface. This causes turbulence and greatly increases drag and reduces down force. A wing should never be used in this situation. In an airplane the point of stall is readily apparent, while in a race car or a kart the point is not so well defined. A sharp reduction in lap times will soon show that the wing is at to severe an angle

Tip Plates. Without tip plates, the airflow will spill over the sides of the wing and create wing tip vortexes. These vortexes increase drag and reduce down force. The portion of the tip plate above the wing is necessary but the size and shape are not very critical. The lower portion is another story. The distance below the wing should be at least three times the chord thickness. The optimum shape for the tip plate is to be wider at the rear than at the front in the sideview. The front should also slope down in a smooth arc.

Flaps or wickerbills are small airfoil sections at the trailing edge of the wing. Since flaps create more down force and little drag at low air speeds they should be given serious consideration for high speed karts.

Aerodynamic balance. It is convenient to have multiple fore and aft wing mounting points to adjust the oversteer/understeer balance aerody-

A very nice and aerodynamically clean package.

namically. If the kart oversteers too much, move the wing back, if it understeers too much, move it forward.

There are several other characteristics of wings, such as Aspect Ratio, which are important to a good design effort but I don't think they are a concern to us in karting yet. If you really want to explore this issue I'm sure a few hours at the local library will be most rewarding.

INITIAL CHASSIS SETUP

The first step in any initial setup is to establish a baseline to work from.

If you've watched much Indy car qualifying I'm sure you've heard the driver say, "Nothing was working right, so we went back to basics". What he means is exactly what it sounds like. They reset the car back to its original baseline.

Every Indy car, and NASCAR team has a detailed layout of exactly how the car was setup before it left the shop, a baseline. Something they can always get back to if the current setting don't work out. The only real difference between them and us is the size of our racing budget.

The baseline can be one of a couple of things. It can be the way the kart is setup now, if your happy with the karts handling, or a complete initial setup starting from the bare frame. This can be done by using the manufacturers recommendations or a general type procedure such as the one presented here. As a rule, it's not necessary to return to a bare frame setup unless you are assembling a new kart, repainting an old one, or making major repairs after an accident. If you are new to karting, it would be best to work with the current setup until you are more comfortable with your capabilities in driving and in understanding how a kart should handle.

The first decision to be made is, should you use the existing setup for a baseline or start completely over? My initial reaction is it's a good idea to record as much of the original setup as possible, use it as an initial baseline, then work with the kart awhile. If you can't get it to handle the way you like, you can start over and create a new baseline. It's kind of like an insurance policy. Something to fall back on if you need to.

If you have a good handling kart, don't rush right out and change everything trying to improve your lap times by a tenth of a second. Chassis setup can be incredibly complex. So many adjustments depend on previous adjustments. Don't be in too big of a hurry to start over. Work with it awhile. Make small changes, keep accurate records of the changes and their effect on the kart. Remember not to be fooled by the seat of the pants feel of the changes. The stopwatch is the only thing that counts.

If you have one of the newer karts with adjustable spindles you can sometimes get some help from the manufacturer. I have talked to a few of them and they assured me that if you bought one of their karts used, and needed help getting it set up, they would be glad to work with you. Most of them

A kart on the surface plate for a check out after an incident on the track.

have printed setup procedures which they make available to new purchasers, as to second and third owners, I don't know. They would not make them available to me for publication, but if requested they would try and help anyone running one of their karts.

CHASSIS ALIGNMENT

The biggest stumbling block to achieving a good setup would be if the frame is misaligned. Chassis misalignment can occur for many reasons. The kart may have been bent in an accident, a front spindle could have been broken, or bent and rewelded, or the frame may be twisted. To check it properly requires a surface plate and a few precision tools. However, there are a couple of preliminary tests you can make to see if the frame is O.K. Insure you do not have any unusual amounts of weight hanging on the frame. Set the kart on a flat level surface. If you have a hanging scale, pick up each front wheel and note the reading required to lift the wheel from the ground. The weight should be within 10 pounds of each other. You can then turn the wheels to the left. The right wheel should be unloaded, measure it. Turn the wheels to the right, the left wheel should be unloaded, measure it. The weight should be within 10 pounds. This not true of a LTO (Left Turn Only), or offset chassis.

Another test to insure that the frame is still square is to measure the wheelbase. Measure from the left kingpin bolt to the center of the rear axle. Write down this measurement and measure the distance from the right kingpin bolt to the center of the right side of the rear axle. Compare the two measurements. The two figures must be the same or else your kart frame may have been bent or incorrectly welded.

If everything seems normal but the kart still does not handle properly, you may decide to strip it down and start completely over. It is not uncommon to dig into this procedure and find a cracked weld or bearing worn oblong.

ESTABLISHING A BASELINE

To establish a baseline for your current kart, I recommend you fill out the baseline worksheet and the weight distribution worksheet included in this book. It is not difficult and it is always nice to have that information to fall back on. I have included copies of these worksheets in the rear of this book so you can tear them out and make copies of them. The following procedure can be used to accomplish this. The information should be compiled for any kart, new or old.

Write down everything even if it's not asked for. You can't make to many notes. To obtain good results you need to do everything the same way every time. All your measurements must be repeatable if you expect to end up with meaningful data.

The first step is to scale the kart. The driver should be in the seat. Insure you have a reasonable amount of air pressure in the tires. 20 pounds rear, 15 pounds front will work for this. Record the weight distribution of all four wheels on the weight distribution worksheet. From this information you can compute the front to rear weight bias as well as left side bias.

The following information should be entered on the chassis baseline chart. Measure the wheel base. This is the distance between the front and rear wheel center to center. Measure the front and rear track. This is the distance between the tires measured from the center of one tire to the center of the other. This is the width of the kart, not the wheelbase. Measure the front toe-in.

Measure the circumference of each tire. One last thing, remove the tires and measure the offset of the wheel halves on all four wheels. Measure from the inside edge of the tire to the center mounting flange. The tire location can be offset by selecting various size wheel halves. The importance of this will be explained later.

Moving to the rear axle, measure the location of the rear hubs. Measure from each hub to the frame bracket. The rear axle bearing has a flange on one side for a set screw which could cause some confusion in this measurement, if you measure

from the bearing itself. It's a good idea to note the bearing orientation but it's best to measure it's actual location from the wheel hub to the frame rail.

Next measure the seat location. The best way to do this is to measure the height of the back lip above the rear axle. Also, measure how far the lip is forward or backward of the axle centerline. Measure the front lip in relation to the closest frame cross member, here again measure the height and location forward and backward. The seat location has a great deal to do with weight distribution and transference of weight during cornering so some care should be used in taking this measurement. Measure the clearance from the bottom of the seat to the ground or the lower edge of the frame rails.

If your seat is mounted using seat struts, it's a good idea to note their location on the frame member and also the tilt forward or backward from the centerline. The reason this is important will be explained later.

Next let's move to the front of the kart. If you have a kart with an adjustable front end, measure the distance between kingpins. You will also need to measure the distance from the kingpin to the front rail on both sides, to determine if the king pins are offset. Measure the left front wheel location on the spindle. Just counting spacers is not good enough. Spacers come in different sizes. Do this by measuring the spacer stack up. Measure the spindle height in the carrier. If all your spacers are the same size you can count spacers here. Measure

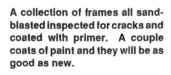

A collection of frames all sandblasted inspected for cracks and coated with primer. A couple coats of paint and they will be as good as new.

the right corner of the kart the same way. The two sides are not necessarily the same. Record current caster settings, if adjustable, and locations of the tie-rod mounting bolts.

After you have done all this you will have a fairly accurate record of your kart as it is now. You should feel good about this, because no matter what happens you can get back to this point.

INITIAL SETUP

This section deals with setting up a kart chassis from a bare frame. I highly encourage you to read through this section even if you are not performing this procedure. There are many points brought out which could be related to your kart. It may give you a few ideas of things you can try to improve the handling of your kart.

If you have been unable to get your chassis to respond the way you think it should or you have a new chassis still in the box, you can use this initial setup procedure to get to a reasonable starting point. If you have manufacturers recommendations, follow them. Most manufacturers have tested their karts and they have a good understanding of what the chassis needs.

If it has not already been done, remove all components from the frame. This includes all bumpers, nerf bars, floor pan and anything that is not welded to the frame.

This picture shows the preferred method of mounting the rear bearing. If you have a long rear axle the cassettes could be mounted on the outside of the frame rail.

The first step is to inspect all the frame welds for cracks. Usually if there is a hair line crack it will be visible. If you suspect a weld but are unsure, heat the area with a torch. If it's really cracked it will heat at different rates and the crack will be readily apparent. Reweld as necessary.

Now is a good time to clean up the frame, perhaps have it sandblasted and put on a new shiny coat of paint. When everything is new and clean it's time to start putting things back together.

REAR AXLE

With a live rear axle you might ask yourself what is there to align? There are a few things to be considered. Should it be mounted offset to the left or right, is it square to the frame and is it bent?

Generally, you can feel a bent axle in your seat. In severe cases the kart will feel like it's going up and down as you drive down the track. One way to check for a bent axle is to measure the rear wheel toe, (if the tires are still mounted on the axle), in the same way as you do the front. Obviously, with a live axle there should be none. If you suspect your axle is bent, the right way to measure it is to mount the axle in a lath or in a pair of Vee blocks and measure the run out with a dial indicator. After the axle is mounted on the kart, you can check for run out with a dial indicator or by clamping a pointer to the frame and rotating the axle.

REAR AXLE MOUNTING

Insure that the rear axle bearings are well oiled and spin freely in their carriers. The axle must not be in a bind. Binding will cause drag, and we all know what drag does for us.

Reinsert the rear axle bearings and bearing cassettes on the axle. I prefer to install the cassette directly above the frame rail. If you have a long axle the cassettes should be mounted on the outside of the frame rails if possible. The axle should slide through both bearings with a minimum amount of resistance.

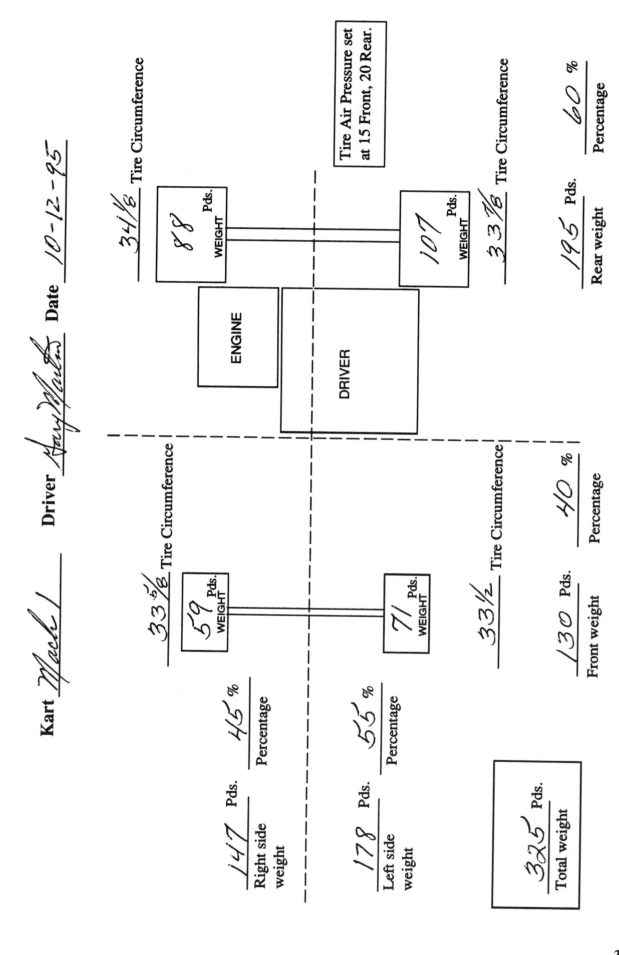

Kart _Mach 1_   Driver _Gary Martin_   Date _10-12-95_

Tire Air Pressure set at 15 Front, 20 Rear.

_34⅛_ Tire Circumference

_88_ Pds. WEIGHT

_107_ Pds. WEIGHT

ENGINE

DRIVER

_33⅞_ Tire Circumference

_195_ Pds. Rear weight

_60_ % Percentage

_33⅝_ Tire Circumference

_59_ Pds. WEIGHT

_71_ Pds. WEIGHT

_33½_ Tire Circumference

_130_ Pds. Front weight

_40_ % Percentage

_45_ % Percentage

_55_ % Percentage

_147_ Pds. Right side weight

_178_ Pds. Left side weight

_325_ Pds. Total weight

WEIGHT DISTRIBUTION WORKSHEET

37

Kart **Mach I**   Date **Gary Martin**

CHASSIS BASELINE WORKSHEET

ENGINE

DRIVER

35" Rear Track

34 1/8" Tire Circumference
3 1/4" Wheel Offset
3 1/4" Hub location

33 7/8" Tire Circumference
3 1/4" Wheel Offset
2 1/2" Hub Location

33 5/8" Tire Circumference
2 1/2" Wheel Offset
1/2" Spindle Height*
15° Caster **
15° Kingpin Inclination**

1 1/2" Hub spacing

1 1/4" Hub spacing

24 3/4" Kingpin spacing

33 1/2" Tire Circumference
2 1/2" Wheel Offset
1/2" Spindle height
15° Caster **
15° Kingpin Inclination**

40 1/2" Wheel Base

34 1/2" Front Track

1/16" Toe-in/out

* Spindle height measured from bottom of bracket

** If adjustable.

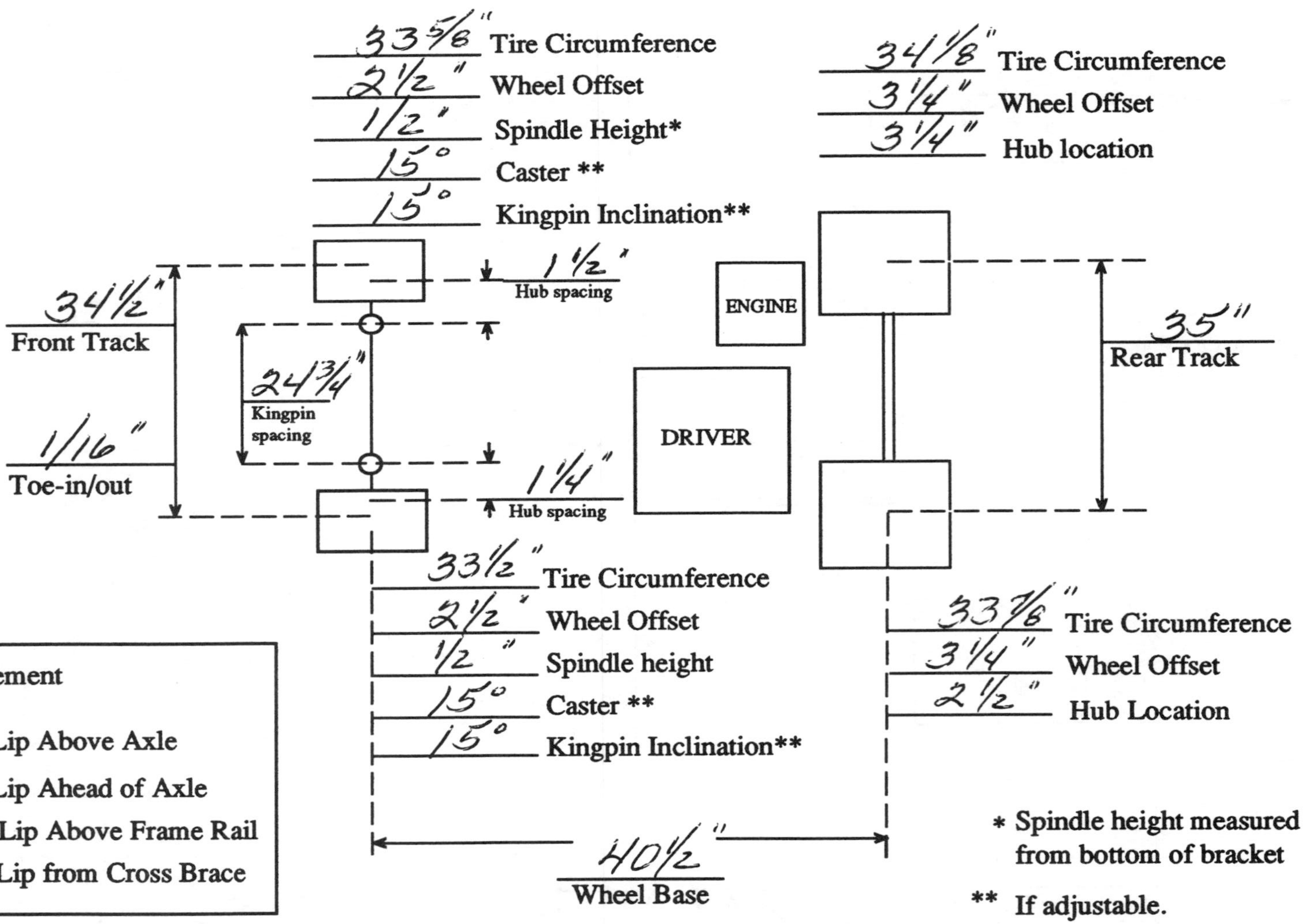

Seat Placement

9" Rear Lip Above Axle
7" Rear Lip Ahead of Axle
2" Front Lip Above Frame Rail
1" Front Lip from Cross Brace

The axle also needs to be square to the frame. With most bearing carriers there is a small amount of play. You can use this play to align the axle. You want the axle square, or ever so slightly forward on the right rear. You can measure this with a framing square or by measuring to the front of the kart. Measure from the tip of the axle to the top center of the kingpin bolt, on both sides. The axle should be centered between the bearings. When the axle is square, tighten the cassette bolts. Slide the axle back and forth. It should still slide easily.

Slide the axle until it comes out of one of the bearings far enough to install the brake disc, and the sprocket hub. Reinsert the axle into the bearing.

Axle location itself is not critical at this time. It is one of those things that will be adjusted at the track. The right rear must have clearance so the tire will not make contact on hard left turns. The left rear should snuggle up against the left side bearing and brake assembly without interference.

Every racer has at one time or another felt a sudden loss of power and initially thought the engine was going to seize up, only to find out later that the wheel or axle had moved, or walked, as it's commonly called, and allowed the tire to rub up against the frame. This can be avoided by securing the axle in the carriers. The two most common methods of securing the rear axle is with locking collars or key stock. Both will be covered here.

Measure the distance from the bearing hangers to the end of the axle on both sides, and insure both dimensions are equal. If you are using locking collars install one on each side of the axle, right up against the bearing. If you put one collar on the inside of the frame rails, make sure they are both on the inside. Do not install the locking collars in a configuration that has one inside and one outside. After the axle locking collars are installed and tighten you should not be able to slide the axle back and forth in the bearings.

Install a length of key stock in each end of the axle. The key stock should be the same length as the channel cut into the axle. This will prevent it from sliding back and forth. If you are using locking collars to secure the rear wheel hubs install them now. Install the rear wheel hubs one inch inboard of the snap rings.

Some of us old dirt racers prefer to secure the axle with key stock. If you are using the key stock method, cut a piece of key stock to fit between the hub and the bearing. I usually place this piece along side the normal key stock. You need to secure both ends of the key stock to keep it in place. I usually put a hose clamp on the hub end and a tie wrap on the bearing end. Put the screw of the hose clamp opposite the key stock to help balance the axle. This does make it a little more difficult to adjust wheel spacing but a hand full of keys cut in 1 or 2 inch steps solves that problem.

I have heard people say the key stock method puts undo strain on the bearing but the truth is a locking collar is pressing against this same surface. I have not had a problem with an axle walking when using the key stock method. Yes, the extra key-stock and hose clamp probably does upset the axle balance a bit but I always felt the extra security of knowing the axle would stay put was worth it, especially on my dirt kart.

The key stock should reach from the hub to the bearing and be secured with tie wraps or a hose clamp.

The brake caliper should be mounted with the bleed valves to the top. This allows the air to raise up to the valves.

BRAKE CALIPERS

Install the two mounting bolts for the brake caliper. Install the calipers with the bleed screws to the top. With the disc between the two halves of the caliper, check to insure the brake pads are not contacting the brake disc. Some brake calipers are adjusted by using shims between the calipers, while others have adjusting screws located in the side of the caliper. New pads should align square. Insure that the clearance is the same top to bottom. Use a feeler gauge and set the pad clearance at .005 to .010 clearance on both sides of the disc. Should you notice a slight angle to the brake pad, check to see if this is caused by the pads or the caliper. If the problem is caused by the pads being worn at an angle, replace the pads. If the problem is the caliper, you can correct this by shimming the area between the caliper and the caliper mounting bracket welded to the frame. Sometimes it only requires taping some shim stock to the outside of the caliper body to straighten its alignment.

If you want more travel in the pedal before you feel the brakes come on you can use a wider pad clearance or install more spacers. If you want brakes as soon as you step on the pedal make the gap as narrow as possible. Be sure the pads don't drag.

GEAR SPROCKET HUB

The sprocket hub is probably as big a concern for karters as anything else on the kart, more races have been lost from chains popping off the sprocket than any other problem. The exact sprocket location can not be determined until we are ready to mount the engine, for now slip the sprocket in place. In most installations you will want the gear and the mounting hardware facing away from the axle bearing.

When the engine is mounted the sprocket hub should be aligned using a straight edge. Insure the hub is secured and cannot walk on the axle.

If the rear tires and wheels are prepared, they can be installed now. Now that you have the rear axle assembly installed, spin the axle to insure that it still rotates freely.

Some chassis have a chain tightening bolt mounted to the rear motor mount cross brace. This bolt is to prevent the motor mount from slipping if the butterflies are not tighten down tight or become loose. If you wish to use this bolt, install it now. Don't forget it's locking nut.

STEERING COLUMN

The steering column should be installed next. First slip the steering column blocks on the shaft and then attach them to their mounts. The aluminum style blocks are preferred, install them with self locking bolts and cotter pins. It's required for safety.

When tightening these bolts, turn the steering shaft to insure you do not have any binding from misalignment. Should there be any binding you might be able to bend the block mounting tabs slightly. When installing the steering wheel, set it in such a way that the spokes of the steering wheel will be at the 6:00, 10:00 and 2 o'clock positions. This will let your hands fit the 4:00 and 8:00 positions without interference from the spokes. It will also allow room for mounting the gauges and night light, if you are using one.

Install long enough bolts in the steering wheel and hub to allow for the mounting of the tach/temp bracket. Install the steering wheel bolts and run safety wire through the mounting bolts. Put cotter pins at both ends of the steering shaft.

SPINDLE INSTALLATION

When beginning to hang the spindles you should first take the kingpin bolts and slide them through the holes in the spindle bracket. The bolt should slide through freely. Inspect the holes in the bracket to insure that they are not worn oblong. The kingpin bolt must be free but close. Next inspect the bearing in each end of the spindle itself. Insure that it is not worn or bound up. Replace as necessary. Many karts have a spindle set up that uses washers to adjust the up and down travel of the spindle. To lower the front of the kart you would put less washers on the top of the spindle than on the bottom. To raise the front of the kart, you would put more washers on top and less on the bottom. If you are running asphalt tracks you want to set the spindle high up in the brackets. This will allow the front to be lower.

Dirt track drivers often change the washers around to fit the banking of certain tracks. Serious dirt karters have adjustable spindles so they don't have to play the washer game. You should test different washer set ups on your home track to see the different results you can obtain. This will be discussed in more detail in the trackside section.

Set both spindles to the same height unless you have a reason to do otherwise. If you do not have a starting point, set the spindle up about 1/2 inch. Install the nut and cotter pin. One more note here is to warn you not to over tighten the kingpin nut. This will put pressure on the spindle bearings and the spindle will be hard to turn. The spindle must rotate freely. Install the tie-rods loosely to the spindles and the steering shaft. If you have a single tie-rod mounting point on the steering column, it is always advisable to install the right tie-rod on the bottom below the left tie-rod. This gives your throttle foot a little more room than it would have if you reversed this set up.

If you look close you can see a adjustment knob on top of the spindle. It will adjust spindle height which affects weight transfer. In dirt racing they are commonly found on both front wheels.

A washer should be installed on each side of the swivel ball in the tie-rod ends. This takes a special type of washer with a small surface area. This will allow the tie-rod ends to pivot without binding. When the steering is at lock, you should be able to take your fingers and rock the tie-rod on the ball.

If you have the type of tie-rods that have a right hand threads on one end and left hand threads on the other you can install the tie-rods and secure the bolts with cotter pins. You will not need to remove the bolts to adjust your toe-in. Should you have the type of tie-rods that have right hand threads on both ends, you should only secure the bolt at the steering column and leave the cotter pin out of the remaining bolts until after the toe-in is adjusted.

An important point to remember when you are measuring for toe-in is to have the bolts holding the tie-rod ends tight. Should the tie-rod bolts be loose when taking these measurements the results will be in error.

BRAKE & PEDAL MOUNTING

Install the brake master cylinder in it's proper location. Make sure you cotter key the nuts. It's not necessary to connect the brake lines until after we mount the pedals.

Install the brake rod between the brake pedal and the master cylinder. Some master cylinders have multiple mounting holes. The upper most hole will allow for more pedal travel. The lower position will give less travel and a harder feel to the pedal. Install the throttle rod to it's pedal. Next jump in the seat and relax. What you want to do now is find a position that allows you the best control of the pedals, while still being relaxed. Check your knee position. The proper leg position should have your knees slightly bent. When you get this position correct, you can then tighten your throttle rod and brake rod jam nuts. Install all cotter pins at this time.

It seems as though all the newer karts have the pedal positions to far forward. I think the trend among younger drivers is to have their legs more stretched out. If you are a little shorter than average, such as I, you may find the pedal position uncomfortable. At least one manufacture has an answer, others may also if you check your local kart shop. Comet Kart Sales has a Enduro style pedal which is straight. It's not curved around as the current style is. I use this type pedal on my sprint kart and it works very well for me.

Moving back to the master cylinder we can now install the brake lines. You will want to fill these lines with brake fluid to aid in the bleeding of the brakes. Fill the master cylinder with brake fluid as well. Be sure to use DOT 5 fluid.

A typical master cylinder installation. Note, the two adjustment holes in the arm. They allow selection of the amount of torque required to apply the brakes.

This is a Enduro style pedal. I prefer it over the curved pedal. It works out better for people with short legs.

Bleeding the brakes can be done in one of two ways. The old style of pump them up and let the air out, or the more recent method of running a line into a bottle of brake fluid. First the pump them up method. If you have air in the lines, pump up the brake pressure and loosen the hydraulic fitting (the brass nut at the caliper). Treat the hydraulic fitting the same as you would a bleeder screw. After bleeding the lines, bleed the caliper using the bleed screw on the calipers. Pump up the pressure with the pedal and open the bleed valve just enough to allow the air to escape. Repeat as often as necessary until the air is out of the system. If you can't get all the air out of the system you may have air in the master cylinder. To bleed it, set the kart in a level position. Most master cylinders do not have a bleed screw on them, but you can still bleed it by using the hydraulic line fittings attached at the rear of the master cylinder.

The more modern means of bleeding the caliper is with a baby bottle and a short piece of 1/4 plastic tubing. Fill the baby bottle about half full of brake fluid. Stick one end of the plastic tube into the brake fluid in the bottle and fill the line itself with brake fluid. Place the other end over the bleed screw. Open the bleed screw and slowly pump the brake pedal until there are no air bubbles coming from the calipers, then close the bleed screw. Repeat this procedure for the other caliper.

Generally the front bumper is mounted ridged to the frame. If your kart is too stiff you can loose up the front by mounting the bumber with rubber grommets.

FRONT BUMPER

The front bumper should be mounted with rubber grommets on the sides. The bumper must be strong enough to take a direct hit, but not so tight it stiffens up the front portion of the frame, and causes the kart to push in the turns.

You should not have to force the bumper and frame holes to line up. If you do it will tighten up the frame. If necessary prebend the arms of the

This innocent looking bolt does more than keep the bumper from falling off. It affects the amount the frame is allowed to flex. Some karts have the bolt mounted the opposite direction so the nuts are showing, but they work the same.

bumper. It's not uncommon for these arms to get bent out of shape because of an accident. This is something that should be checked from time to time especially if you have been in a tangle and find the handing of the kart has changed.

REAR BUMPER

There are several different methods of attaching the rear bumper. No matter what type you have it's important for you to realize that the rear bumper is another one of thoses torsion bars we talked about. How rigided its mounted affects chassis handling.

Many of the karts on the market today use a large bolt and rubber bushing which slide up inside the fram rail. Frame flex is controlled by how tight the bolt or nut is tightened.

Install the rear bumper by pushing the bolts and rubber bushing into the rear of the frame rails. For now tighten the rear bumper bolts to 100 inch pounds. This is considered a loose setting. If we wanted to tighten up the kart we would tighten the bolts to 200 inch pounds. The important thing for now is that they be tightened the same. We will discuss bumper adjustment in greater detail in "Trackside".

SEAT INSTALLATION

Seat position is one of the most important steps in kart handling because it effects center of gravity, weight distribution, and weight transfer. You can probably get a hundred different ideas of how to do this. I can only tell you what works for me and what I see being done. You should setup your kart and do a little experimenting to find out what works best for you.

Install the right seat brace loosely to the rear cross bar. If you are planning on running asphalt, install the left seat brace on the cross bar as well.

Karts being set up for dirt or oval racing should consider a left seat brace that is made to clamp to the left side rail of the kart. This will allow you to mount the seat more to the left. This will give you more left side weight. On most tracks this would give you the desirable inside weight advantage for handling on loose tracks.

Place your seat between the frame rails so that the front center portion of the seat is up against the steering posts. This initial step will give you as much up front weight as allowed by the kart. On dirt karts you would want to set the seat to the most forward position and the farthest to the left as the steering post will allow. You may find after testing the, the seat will need to be notched so it can be moved further forward.

Mark and drill the holes to match the front seat mounts. Install the bolts loosely and prop up the seat so that you can sit on it without it collapsing. Usually, setting the kart on a flat surface with a 3/4 or 1 inch piece of wood under the seat will work. Remember we want to keep it as low as possible.

Choosing the proper incline of the seat depends on comfort as well as the type of racing. For dirt tracks the trend is to use a more setup posistion, while, asphalt sprint tracks favor a more reclined position. A word of caution here is not to get too radical on reclining your seat. What you want is a position that feels comfortable and allows you to grab the steering wheel at the 4 and 8 positions with your elbows tucked into your sides. From this position you need to be able to move the steering wheel without your elbows getting into the engine.

A well positioned seat mount. Also note rear torsion bar is set for max stiffness.

When you decide the proper amount of recline you want, bring the seat struts up against the seat. Mount the right rear seat strut so that the top mounting hole is ahead of the lower frame mounting end. You want any body weight being transferred from the seat to push against the frame member. Insure that the seat strut will not interfere with the proper operation of the clutch. Mark and drill the holes. The bolts attaching the seat to the seat strut should have a rubber grommet between the seat and the strut. As you tighten the bolts watch to see that the seat is not in a bind. A bind here will also create a bind in the frame that will translate into a handling problem on the track. Tighten all bolts at this time.

FLOOR PAN

If you want a tight kart, mount the floor pan directly to the frame mounting tabs. This will tighten up the frame rails and take some of the flex out of the frame. If you prefer a loose frame enlarge the mounting holes in your floor pan to insure all the bolts will slide through the holes without interference. Use bolts that are longer than the original bolts. Install the bolts from the bottom side of the floor pan, place a rubber grommet between the floor pan and the tab. Use a self locking nut to secure the bolt, do not tighten the nut more than enough to hold the floor in place.

If you are running a 4-cycle, do not install the pan mounted fuel tank supplied with some karts. Some karters like to use this tank to add weight, by adding fuel or water to the tank. This is bad for several reasons. First it makes the weight too high on the kart. Second, if the tank isn't full, the load will be shifting from corner to corner, and third the tank mounting arrangement is less than satisfactory for carrying extra weight. In time the bolts will fracture the floor pan. If you are racing 2-cycles and need to use the pan mounted tank, you should use very large washers on both sides of the floor pan to help spread the weight over the largest area possible. It's best to replace the skinny spacers with larger blocks, if you can find some. There are some after market spacers available to do that job.

Side pods and nerf bars can be used to stiffen the frame. If the frame is too stiff rubber grommets should be used between the bars and the frame.

NERF BARS

If you have the type of kart that has its nerf bars attached with tube stubs you will find that the nerf bars are held in place with a bolt going through the tube. With a drill slightly enlarge the hole in the nerf bar so that when the bolt is tight the nerf bar can flex up and down. What we are trying to accomplish is the same thing we did with the rear bumper. We want it to stay on to protect ourselves, but not to stiffen the frame flex.

Should you have the type of frame that has a tab with a bolt through it, install a rubber grommet between the tab and nerf bar to help with the flex. In either case, use a bolt long enough to install a self locking nut or a cotter key without it being fully tight.

WEIGHT DISTRIBUTION

At this point we have the frame pretty well back together. The last major effort is to set the weight distribution. Before we do that we will need to mount the wheels and engine, if they are not mounted. The wheels and the tires should have

been prepared as outlined in the chapter on tires. The engine should be mounted complete with clutch and pipe to obtain proper weight distribution numbers.

The sprocket and chain should also be installed at this time. Be sure to align the sprocket with the drive gear on the clutch. This can be done with a steel straight edge. Insure that the sprocket is secure, so it cannot walk on the axle.

Most karters add weight to the front floor pan or bumper without regard for weight distribution. It's easy to assume that with the engine weight on the right rear, any extra weight should be added to the left rear.. The truth is, in the adult classes, the driver usually makes up the biggest share of the weight. Most asphalt karts have too much left rear weight because the driver sits left of center. If we are going to be successful at this karting thing, we will need to set the weight bias for the type of racing we plan to do. For an asphalt road course we want to start with about 40/60 front to rear and 55/45 left side/right side bias, for oval racing we can increase the left side weight even more.

Before you actually measure your karts weight distribution, you need to perform a few preliminary setups. Insure that you have the correct air pressure in the tires. If at all possible, you should use the tires you expect to use for the kart setup. For measurement purposes put 15 pounds in the front tires and 20 pounds in the rear.

Next measure the circumference of the tires using either a cloth tape measure or a very narrow steel tape. Measure around the center of the tire. You can write the measurement on the side of the tire with chalk. The measurements should be reasonably close to each other. Within 1/2 inch. If one tire is unusually big or small you should replace it, unless you are setting up for a oval or dirt track and you know you will be running a lot of stagger. I personally prefer to set my weight balance with a neutral kart. Mount the smallest rear tire on the left rear and the smallest front tire on the left front. Even if you are road racing, most of the tracks have more left turns than rights.

To measure weight distribution you should have 4 scales. You can do it with two or even one but it goes a lot easier with four. Bathroom scales will work but platform scales work best. You can usually pick these up at auctions. **45**

Some people advocate that you should only use one scale. If you use only one scale you must block up the other 3 corners of the kart so the kart will set level. The problem I have with using one scale is that it takes 4 times as long to scale the kart.and everytime you make a change you have to go back around the kart to get the new measurements. Thing just go so much smoother with four scales.

The first step is to insure the scales themselves are all the same height and level with each other. Level across all four scales from front to back and side to side.

The scales should then be calibrated to insure they read properly. You can use a 80 pound bag of softer salt or a 90 pound bag of cement for the rears and a 40 pound bag of salt for the front scales. Measure your fixed weight on all four scales. It should read within 2 pounds on all four scales. The exact weight is not necessarily important, but they must weigh the same. Most scales can be adjusted by adding or removing weight from the weight hanger. After everything is O.K., recheck the scales with your own body weight. Now the fun part. Place the kart on the scales so that each wheel is located in the center of each scale. The driver should be in the kart and the measurements taken. Enter the weight on one of the setup forms. We can now analyze the information to see what we have and what needs to be done.

The ideal weight distribution is a matter of choice. I can only say that I initial set my kart up for 55/45 left side/right side and 40/60 front/back and fine tune from there. I feel that it's a good base line. You may elect to do otherwise. These are not hard fast guide lines.

With this in mind lets see what you should have. With a 325 pound kart you should have numbers similar to those shown in figure 6. A quick analysis of the numbers for your kart will show where improvement can be made.

Now that we know where the weight is, what can we do about it? The biggest gains in this respect is in the location of the seat. Move the seat left, right, front to back to obtain the desired results.

In most cases, any weight that must be added to make racing weight will need to be added at the left front corner. It should be added as close to the spindle as possible without interfering with the steering control arms. I have added 35 pounds to meet stock heavy weight, so I know it can be done and still achieve a well balanced kart.

If you can not get the front distribution right, you may need to raise or lower the spindle in the spindle bracket. This is done by moving washers from top to bottom or vice versa. If the left front is too light, raise the right front spindle or lower the left front. You should not have to make too great a change here. Work from side to side, first one side than the other. If a lot of adjustment is required it

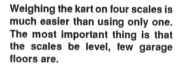

Weighing the kart on four scales is much easier than using only one. The most important thing is that the scales be level, few garage floors are.

If the track you race at has digital scales, they can tell you the weight on each wheel. It's displayed on their monitor automatically. If you go up and weigh sometime when their not busy they will give you that information.

may be an indication the frame is tweaked. Usually it is only necessary to adjust the spindles if you are measuring dynamic weight transfer.

While we are sitting on the scales we can get an idea of the amount of weight that will be transferred when we turn into a corner. Mount a degree wheel in the center of the steering wheel. With the front wheels pointed straight ahead set a pointer to "0" degrees. Now turn the steering wheel 17 degrees to the left. Read the measurements on the four scales. This should show that 10% of the original weight has been transfer to the right rear wheel. This is weight jacking as explained in the theory section.

There are for the most part only two things which affect the amount of this weight transferance. Spindle geometry, and frame stiffness. If you are setting up a stiff frame for dirt tracking or a small oval, you should be transferring less weight to the right. A more flexible frame will transfer more weight.

You can observe the effects of stiffening up the frame by tightening up one of the torsion bars or adding an extra brace to the seat and repeating the measurements. You should see an decrease in the amount of weight transferred. If the kart has left side weight bias when you repeat this procedure for the right turn, you will find somewhat less weight transfer because of this bias.

If you intend to add weight to the chassis by filling the frame with lead, I suggest you fill the frame full. This method does get the weight very low on the chassis which is good. However, if the frame is not full the weight bais has a tendency to change with the motion of the kart.

If you are using this initial setup as your baseline, take the time to go back and fill out the baseline worksheet. We will probably want to modify it a little, after a few trips to the track, but we want a record of where we stand.

Well there you have it. A reasonably well setup, rolling chassis. Now we can get ready for a trip to the track.

TRACKSIDE

Finally we get to the good part. I don't know about you, but for me, all the time, money and hard work seems insignificant when you drive out onto the track. When you take off the mechanics hat and put on the helmet, it's all worth while. The time on the track is without a doubt the most enjoyable part of karting. All the long hours and money spent all seems worthwhile when your making laps. The only fly in the ointment is you just spent in excess of $500.00 for that new blue printed engine and your lap times are not any better.

I hate to cloud your picture more but perhaps you were looking for the speed in the wrong place. In most of the controlled classes of kart racing the engines have reach a fairly high degree of precision. There is not a lot of difference between engines, assuming they're all legal. The chances are far more likely that the secret of lower lap times will be found in improving chassis handling. The ability to fine tune the chassis is perhaps the most overlooked aspect of racing. Most karters just try and force the kart around the track with horsepower instead of getting to the heart of the matter.

As you go about the process of setup and dialing in the kart, remember everybody and every kart is different. You want your kart to feel good to you. What someone else is doing should only be considered as reference material. Remember when you get to the track, it's your kart, you have to make it work for you. Don't be afraid to try new things. That is what practice is for. Working the kart through the paces can take a considerable amount of time, but you should see steady improvement along the way. You should never be completely satisfied with your setup. You should always be doing some fine tuning. Always trying to improve. By all means keep a record so you can back track if necessary.

This chapter is divided into three sections. Practice day tuning, race day tuning and tje race. No matter what type of racing you are participating in, asphalt, dirt, oval, or just for fun, you should find some things here that will help you dial in that chassis. Some of the things unique to dirt racing are presented in a later chapter titled "Dirt Racing". Let's get down to business.

It's best to sort out the handling on a practice day, as race days are just too limited time wise for anything but fine tuning for existing track and weather conditions. Most all of the things tried during practice could be tried on race day, but I have found that because of the limited time, you usually end up changing several things at once and before you know it you don't know what worked and what didn't. Also we tend to be a little more conservative on race day because we don't want to lose the handle on things.

Now that we're at the track, our bag of tricks is down to a manageable level. Everything major has been done and we only need to dial in the chassis. We can adjust front or rear track, spindle height, tire air pressure, reposition weight, or adjust the stiffness of the frame. Five easy steps to better handling.

Don't forget the objective of the practice session is to get the kart around the corner at the maximum speed possible. Except for overpowered dirt karts, you should avoid pitching the kart sideways to steer it through the corner with the back end. A kart will scrub off a lot of speed when it is pitched sideways, and it will take several seconds to get the momentum back up. In the meantime, a driver with his kart properly setup, driving his kart around the corner will gain 3 to 4 kart lengths. This is especially true in stock 4-cycle racing.

Don't be in a hurry to try things. You need to take your time and work in small planned steps. Before you set out onto the track, set your initial tire air pressure, 20 rears and 15 fronts with the tires cold.

I usually run a session of seven or eight laps, take fifteen or twenty minutes to make a change and then run another session. Remember you are not here just to put laps on the motor. I do not believe it's necessary to run a lot of consecutive laps. Over the years I have found that my fastest laps are almost always the fourth or fifth lap. For some people the first or second lap may be the fastest one. After you've done some serious testing, look over

your times and I think you will see a pattern develop. Then you'll know how many laps it takes to get into the rhythm.

First I like to run a few laps without timing myself to get some heat into the engine and tires. The second time out, I time myself and use this for the official starting point. If you are running a 4-cycle, don't forget to do things like changing oil and checking for broken dippers.

Now it's time to decide what problems you are going to attack. In big car racing where they have big sweeping turns it's easy to determine how a car handles going into, through, and coming out of a corner. In most forms of kart racing this all happens so fast that it's hard to distinguish the difference. It's probably best to just worry about the entrance and exit of the turns.

Some people have a natural ability to understand what is happening to the chassis and others don't. If you are having trouble in this respect, take it one corner at a time. Remember a corner has two important parts as far as kart handling is concerned, an entrance and a exit. Drive through the corner in question as hard as you feel you can and ask yourself what is preventing you from negotiating the corner faster. If you're still in doubt try going a little faster. It's best to do this when you are alone on the track so you don't have to worry about someone getting into you if you get a little cross ways.

This kart is tranfering too much weight to the right rear. It has lifted the left front off the track. The kart could use some right front weight. It takes a good driver to steer a kart when only one wheel is doing all the steering.

The leading kart here is in the proper grove as shown by the rubber and wear on the track. The trailing kart is much to high and in danger of getting into the loose stuff which collects on the outside of the turns. The trailing kart could be understeering however, the front wheels do not indicate the kart is being turned down to the apex.

We will cover some of the more common handling problems that we might have encountered during our first. practice session and see what we can do to correct them. Following these you will find several adjustments that can be made to the kart and what effect they have on kart handling.

The two most common problems mentioned when discussing kart handling is understeer and oversteer. Understeer simply means when you turn the front wheels the kart wants to continue going in a straight line. This is quite often referred to as pushing. Oversteer means when you turn the wheels the kart comes right on around usually sliding the back end out. This is quite often referred to as loose, however, a kart can be loose without having an oversteer problem with the front. We will cover some of the causes and cures for these conditions.

PUSHING/UNDERSTEER

The most likely problem we will encounter is a pushing problem. When the front wheels are turned the kart wants to continue to go straight. Understeer is usually caused by the front tires not getting enough bite. Before we start working on the chassis, let's be sure we understand the tires' position in this. I hope you have read the chapter on tires. If not, you should do so. The front tires have the most effect on understeer. The tires contribution to understeer is caused by two conditions, old, hard tires and tires that are of a hard compound. If you are going to race with new tires each race day, you should setup the kart with new tires. If like most of us you run a set of tires three or four race days, you should use tires that have a couple of races on them for the setup. If you setup the chassis with old tires and then put on new ones, the chassis will have more bite. If you setup with new tires and race with old tires the chassis will become loose. If you are using an older set for setup you may need to run a few hard laps to get them up to working temperature before you start tuning your chassis. You will find that the kart understeers for four or five laps and then starts to come around. The older a tire gets the longer,(more laps), it takes for the tires to come around. Hard compound tires do not change as drastically as old tires, but they still change. If you are racing these same tires, or run a class that requires a hard compound tire you must decide if you want to setup the kart for the first few laps, or the last few. Usually it's best to compromise for somewhere in between. In kart racing the first few laps seem to be the most important.

If the kart has a pushing problem the type of adjustment to be made depends on where the push takes place.

Kart pushes in both left and right hand turns.
Let's take an example of a kart that pushes in both left and right hand turns. Insure that the front tire air pressure is not too high. The pressure should be approximately 15 pounds. Try reducing the air pressure a couple of pounds in both front tires. Next, try widening the rear track, at this point you can move the wheels out about an inch at a time. If you were fine tuning on race day you would only use 1/2 inch steps. Don't worry about the WKA rule, that the tires must be inside the side nerf bars. We want to make the kart handle properly first. If we need to space out the nerf bars later we can do that. The next step would be to move both front wheels in one spacer.

If you still have the push you may need to add more forward weight. This means you will have to either add weight to the front of the kart or move the seat forward. If the problem persists it may be necessary to notch your seat so you can move it forward even further. The next step would be to lower the front of the kart by raising the front spindles in their brackets.

Kart pushes in one direction only. If your kart only pushes in one direction the first step is to check the tire air pressure, tire stagger and spindle height. If all is O.K., move the front wheel, opposite the push, in on the spindle. If the kart pushes when you turn left, (kart wants to continue straight), you would move the right front wheel in on its spindle.

The seat position can also be a big reason for pushing in one direction. Your body weight has more influence on weight distribution than any other factor. Sometimes the addition of five or ten pounds of weight on a corner of the kart can help solve a one direction pushing problem. If the kart pushes on left turns, add weight to the right front corner. On dirt you will probably find over half the karts out there are using additional weight to help steer around the corners better.

Kart pushes on corner entry. Too little front end weight. Move weight to the front of the kart. Widen rear track width. If the kart is pushing going into a left turn, the kart is too tight on the right rear. Space the right rear wheel out, or take some right rear weight out of the kart. Move the weight to the

front. Some other things you can do are; add more stagger, put on new tires, add toe-out, decrease front stagger, or loosen up the front bumper.

Kart pushes on corner exit. Too little front end weight. Move weight forward on the chassis, tires too hard, either because of a hard compound or old age. If this is the problem you will find the understeer will improve as the tires heat up. Change to softer or new tires. Too much tire air pressure in the front causing the tire contact patch to be rounded instead of flat. Reduce air pressure. Front tire track too wide, move tires closer together. Add air pressure to the right rear tire, add toe in, add stagger to rear, move left front out.

Other solutions would be the same as those in corner entry, and if they don't work go back and raise the spindle. If you adjust the spindle height be sure to reset the toe-in. Moving the spindle will upset the tie-rod arc. Another more serious cause could be the frame is tweaked so that one tire or the other is not getting a good bite.

OVERSTEER

Another condition you may experience is oversteer. Oversteer is actually hard to detect because so many things mask it. This is when the front bite of the kart is so good the kart darts into the corner. This often results in the rear of the kart breaking loose, which usually leads to a spin out.

Most karters do not associate the rear end being loose with oversteer. While they are similar in results, they are different problems. The rear of the kart can be loose without the kart oversteering, although it's sometimes hard to tell the difference.

I'm not sure how prevalent oversteer is in karting. Being loose in the rear is very common, whether caused by oversteer or other reasons. The problem is to determine if you should work on the front to cure oversteer or on the rear to cure the loose condition. So how do you know where to start?

Usually it's best to get the rear of the kart settled down, then sort out oversteer. Then when you have oversteer corrected, go back and loosen up the rear end until it's the way you like it.

Oversteer is most noticeable when you turn into the corner and then find yourself over correcting back the opposite direction for a second, and then turning back into the turn. You may not even realize you are doing this at first. Obviously this is not the fastest way around the corner. You have to be smooth if you want to be fast.

Oversteer is caused by the front tires getting too much bite. It usually manifest itself first in excess wear of the front tire. It can be caused by too little air pressure in the front tire or too soft of a tire compound. Add air pressure or change to a harder compound. Front tire track may be too narrow. It can also be caused by too much front end weight. In this case move some weight to the rear. Next move the rear track in. Spindle height may be miss adjusted, or the frame is tweaked.

REAR OF KART LOOSE

Another handling problem you may find is known as a loose kart. This is where the back end of the kart slides out while tuning a corner. The front end of your kart sticks pretty good, but the back end wants to come around.

Usually, a kart that is loose can be remedied by one of two things. The first thing you should do is bring the rear wheels in on the axle. Under practice conditions you can start with 1 inch increments. The more you bring in the rear wheels, the less bite the front end will have, which may cause understeer (pushing in the front). If you reach this point move the wheels back out.

You can also adjust the rear tire air pressure. Reduce the air pressure in both rear tires. If you have to reduce the pressure below 10 pounds you need to look for another answer.

Many dirt drivers like running tire pressures so low the bead of the tire barely seats. Their reasoning is the smaller amount of pressure will give them better grip. They are correct to a degree, but like in all racing there must be a compromise. Low air pressure will also cause a tire to roll in a turn, which actually causes the kart to transfer more weight, which will pull the tire from it normal tracking.

The next step is to add more flex to the frame so it will transfer more weight to the right rear. This can be done by loosening up the rear bumper or if your kart has a rear mounted torsion bar. Rotate the flat part of the torsion bar to the flat position.

If the kart is loose entering the corner add toe-in, narrow rear track width, add air to right front tire, decrease air in right rear tire, decrease rear stagger. Loosen rear bumper. Lower rear axle in chassis.

If the kart is loose on corner exit, reduce rear stagger, move right rear tire in, reduce rear tire air pressure, Lower rear axle in chassis, softer tires or new tires. If the kart is loose on dry/slick track, the kart needs more rear weight. Adjust it evenly to the rear end. Raising up the nose of the kart will also add more weight to the rear.

Usually being slightly loose coming off a corner is not all bad as long as it's not excessive. After a few laps the tires will heat up and it will come off the corner just right. If you tighten the chassis up when the tires are cold you may end up with oversteer or bicycling when the tires get hot in the closing laps, and this will hurt your turn speed. The lower the horsepower, the looser the kart needs to be coming off the turn.

Two rules to remember. The wider the rear track the more likely you are to be loose in the rear. The narrower the rear track the better the rear end will stick.

Another common problem is rear end hop. When you make a hard left hand turn and the rear

HOPPING OR BICYCLING

of the kart wants to bounce or skitter. This may be solved by moving the right rear wheel out approximately 1 inch. The same holds true if the kart hops in right hand turns. Move the left wheel out approximately 1 inch. Do not worry about the kart not being square. The important thing is to get the chassis to handle properly.

Hopping can also be improved by increasing tire air pressure, a couple of pounds at a time to the rear corner, opposite to the direction of the turn. Hopping could also occur if you have excessive stagger.

If the hopping is only noticeable in one certain turn, it may be caused by a ripple or bump in the track. Walk the corner when you have a chance to verify this. You should not try to correct for that. You can try to avoid the rough spot but more often than not, it's in the groove. You can reduce tire air pressure to soften the effects of the bump, but watch your lap times.

If a kart bicycles, (outside tires have too much bite, inside tires lift off the ground) try adjusting tire air pressure. If front and rear both come off the ground together, increase both front and rear track. If this doesn't help, increase tire pressure in the side with excessive bite. Move right rear further out on the axle or switch to a harder compound tire.

This is called bicycling. It is not the fast way around the corner. The kart has too much bite. The quick fix is more tire air pressure. Next would be moving the outside tires out on the axle, or by reducing frame flex.

VEERING

Veering is when the kart wants to pull to one side when you are trying to go in a straight line. To determine if your kart is veering, all you have to do is let go of the steering wheel while you are headed in a straight line. If the kart starts to veer off to the left or right you have a veering condition. One of the main causes of veering is tire stagger.

Tire stagger in asphalt racing should be minimal. Excessive stagger will help a kart corner quicker to that direction but it will also add drag to your straightaway speed and will make turns in the opposite direction really difficult. You should setup the kart with a near neutral setting. I realize

that you are somewhat stuck with the tires you get from the dealer, but ideally for asphalt road courses you would like to start with 1/4 inch or less stagger. For ovals or dirt tracks you may want 2 or 3 inches.

Another possibility to check is to see if any of the wheel bearings are dragging. Put the kart on a kart stand and give the wheels a spin. They should spin freely. Another possibility for a kart that wants to veer is a sprung kart frame. See the Sprung frame section later in this chapter.

DARTING

Darting is defined as a kart that twitches or darts at the slightest movements of the steering wheel.

To correct a darting condition check your toe-in. If that does not correct the problem you could also check the tie-rod mounting points on the spindle arms. If you can, move the tie-rod ends to a pair of holes farther out on the arms. This would slow down the steering. For further information on toe, refer to toe-in in the theory section. For further information on tie-rod location refer to the section on Ackerman steering.

Thus far we have covered some common problems and what you can do to correct them. Now we will cover some adjustments that are available to you at the track and what their effect on the karts handling will be. You may also wish to refer to the handy quick reference guide on pages 77 & 78 for further ideas of things to try.

TIRE TRACK

Tire track (the distance between tires, kart width, not wheel base) is one adjustment which can be made to compensate for a pushing or loose condition. You can widen or narrow the front track width by moving the wheels in or out with different

54

wheel spacers or by using different wheel offsets. At the rear, the wheels can be spaced in or out along the axle by moving the hubs.

Wider front track will cause the front end to push more. The steering will be slower and somewhat harder. You will transfer more weight to the rear wheels. A narrower front track width will cause the front end to bite more. The steering will feel quicker and easier. You will transfer less weight to the rear when turning. When this happens, it loosens up the rear end. If the rear track width of the kart is narrower than the front, it will keep more weight in the left rear and create more side bite on the right rear during corning.

Narrowing the rear, will give you more side bite. Kart will push more, (bite less) in the front. Wider rear, rear end will bite less and the front will push less, (more bite in the front).

STAGGER ADJUSTMENTS

The more stagger the kart has the less bite it will have. Air pressure and tire temperature variations effect stagger most, followed closely by tire wear. If stagger increases, you lose rear bite and will develop a loose or oversteer condition. In longer races the less stagger the better.

Weight should not be just haphazardly added. Its placement should depend on weight distribution and kart handling.

Always measure stagger hot and cold. This way you will know how much your tires will grow during a race. Just because tires are of the same brand and compound does not mean they have the same circumference. Measure them, every tire is different.

On a road course start with zero stagger and increase stagger 1/8 or 1/4 inch at a time until your lap times begin to drop off. Most well behaved karts will not want much more than that. On dirt or an oval track you can start with 1 inch and work up from there. Remember to watch your lap times. Don't just go by the feel of the kart.

WEIGHT ADJUSTMENT

Side bite determines how fast a racer can enter and get around a turn. The outside two wheels need to be predominant around the turn. We want to transfer just enough weight to the outside wheels to induce side bite. Side bite helps overcome the natural tendency of the kart to first under and then oversteer as it goes through a turn. The trade off for side bite is at the expense of forward traction.

The rule of thumb, is the more horsepower, the more rear weight percentage you can run. More rear weight allows more balanced braking, and more even tire wear because the weight is more evenly spread over the rear tires. Maximum forward acceleration occurs when rear weight is equally divided between each rear wheel.

Too much rear weight can cause the front of the kart to push. For asphalt racing, try and keep the weight at the 60/40 ratio set when the kart was scaled. For dirt racing move the weight rear ward as long as you don't lose front bite.

In regards to left side/right side weight balance, on flat, slow tracks keep the left/right percentage near equal. For banked tracks move the weight to the left. On high bank increase the left side percentage, and reduce rear percentage.

Weight transfer can also be controlled by caster and spindle settings. This was explained more fully in the chapter on chassis theory. The more caster the more a chassis tuning to the left is unloaded. Bite is taken out of the kart turning to the left. Less caster adds bite.

REAR STEER

Rear steer is defined as the condition where the rear end is shifted forward slightly on the right side to gain a touch more bite exiting the turns, and/or shifted rearward to help the kart entering the turns under braking. Under certain conditions rear steer does help bite, but only with a trade off in other areas. Overall, rear steer may help, but at the cost of straight-away stability, especially on rough tracks. Most karts today do not permit adjusting rear axle alignment. It's best to setup the kart neutral, unless you have time to experiment with this.

TIRE AIR PRESSURES

The lower the air pressure the larger the contact patch which in turn gives better tire grip. Lower air pressure is used in situations where more bite is required, or bite is hard to get, such as on a real dry/slick track or a very smooth cement track. Excessively low tire pressure gives the kart a squirrely, or fish tail effect because the tires sidewalls can no longer support the kart. Air pressure is discussed in more detail in the race day activity section a little later.

WHEEL OFFSET

The offset of a wheel is measured from the wheel center to the inner edge of the rim. The further the wheel is out, the less weight on it. For instance, on the right rear, the greater the offset, the looser the kart will be entering a corner. The less offset, the tighter the kart will be entering a corner. Also, the kart will exit a corner faster with less right rear offset. The closer the right rear is tucked in toward the center of the kart, the better the forward traction of the kart.

The front wheel offset can also be changed to loosen the kart up or make it push a little more. For instance, if the kart starts with a 1 1/2-inch offset wheel at the right front, and then a 2 1/2-inch offset wheel is installed (which pushes the wheel outward 1-inch), this may cause the kart to push. consequently offsetting the wheel in tighter will reduce the push. The further the tire is tucked in toward the center of the kart, the tighter it will make the kart.

TRACK CONDITIONS

If we're racing on Oct. 10th. at a particular track, you must remember that this set of conditions will never occur exactly the same again. Keeping records of particular tracks is good as long as a racer realizes he must always adjust to the weather and track conditions. You must never be completely satisfied. You can always make it go a little faster if you try.

CHASSIS FLEX

The flexibility of the frame can be adjusted on practice and race days. The mechanisms for doing this are the rear torsion bar, rear bumper, and one or more of the new adjustment methods explained in the section on chassis.

The chassis flex on this kart is adjustable while in motion. If you look real close you can see the adjustment knob located between the tires.

Some of the newer frames on the market are of great concern to me. I realize the manufactures are attempting to build a flexible frame for handling reasons. But I really have to wonder how they will stand up to the abuse of weekly racing. What is going to happen the first time a kart like this is involved in an accident. Note the weight added to the front bumper. That is not a very good idea, and in fact some clubs do not allow it.

Whichever means you use to change the frame stiffness the results are basically the same. The stiffer the frame, the less weight transferred and the less bite the rear will have.

SPRUNG FRAME

If you are still having problems getting the kart to handle properly, perhaps the frame is sprung. To determine if the frame is sprung, place the kart on a flat surface. Lift either front wheel and note the amount of lift it takes to get it off the ground. Now lift the other front wheel and note any difference. This is not true with LTO and offset chassis. If there is none, your frame is probably O.K. on this count. If there is a difference, your frame has probably been sprung, either from a crash or from running the same track for a considerable amount of time. The metal in the frame tends to become accustomed to giving in one direction and eventually the metal begins to retain the twisting, caused by the turns. This in simple words is a sprung frame.

There is no correct fix for this. You could send the frame back to the factory and have it realigned, but who is really going to do this unless it's a brand new frame. There is a way to flex the frame back to somewhere near it's original shape. However, it will never be as good as new and it will continually

spring as time goes on. Get a jack stand and place it under the wheel that was the heaviest to lift. Have someone stand on the rear tire on the same side as the jack stand. Now jump with a good degree of bounce on the front wheel of the side that is not supported by the stand. One or two good bounces should do the trick. Remove the kart from the stand and check the wheel lift technique again. If it's still not right repeat the procedure. This may not be very scientific but it will improve the handling at least for a while.

RACE DAY TUNING

Hopefully when you get to race day most of your work is done. With the limited practice time available it's just not possible to make wholesale changes at this time. At this point you should be able to fine tune the kart with tire air pressure, stagger or wheel location, and moving a few pounds here and there.

Operating under the assumption that the basic setup is close, we should start with tire air pressure.

I recommend you set the air pressure when you arrive at the track, with the tires cold, before you start making laps. Unless you have a preferred starting point, put 20 pounds in the rears and 15 pounds in the fronts. Some tire brands require more, some less, but you need a starting point. Start from here each race day. After making a few laps to heat up the rubber, you can make a decision on how to adjust the tire air pressure.

Do not worry about constantly reading the tire air pressure. I've seen some karters check their air pressure before and after every race. This is not necessary and may in fact be detrimental. You should remember the air pressure will change with the temperature. The pressure may be 3 or 4 pounds higher when you come off the track, so unless you read it at exactly the same time every time, your readings will fluctuate throughout the day. Also remember the volume of air in a kart tire is not very great. Every time you measure the air pressure you let some air out. This may be as much as a pound if you are not careful.

Knowing the exact amount of air in the tires is not important because you will be adjusting it after every race to improve the handling for the next race.

During the first practice session you must analyze the chassis handling. Insure you have the tires heated up to operating temperature before making any decisions. If you are running a hard compound or old tires this may take a few laps.

If the kart does not have any serious pushing, understeer, or oversteer problems, which it won't have if you prepared it properly, adjust the tire air pressure this way.

If the rear is loose on both left and right turns, let air out of both rears. If the rear is loose only on left hand turns, let air out of the right rear. If the rear is loose only on right hand turns, let air out of the left rear.

If the rear bites too much (hops or bicycles) on both left and right turns, add air to both rears. If the rear bites too much only on left hand turns, (hops or bicycles), add air to only the right rear. If the rear bites too much only on right hand turns, (hops or bicycles), add air to only the left rear.

If the front pushes on both left and right hand turns, let air out of both fronts. If the front pushes only on left hand turns, let air out of the right front. If the front pushes only on right hand turns, let air out of the left front.

If the front oversteers on both left and right turns, add air to both front tires. If the front oversteers only on the left hand turns, add air to the right front. If the front oversteers only on right hand turns, add air to the left front.

As a rule you should not need to adjust the air pressure more than a few pounds, unless you are operating under extreme weather conditions. The rears should be between 15 and 25 except for maybe some dirt racing. The fronts should be between 10 and 20 for a norm. If you can't dial in the kart with these pressures, you need to change the kart track (the spacing on the rear wheels, or the front spindle spacers) as explained in Tire Track earlier in this section.

If the chassis has a tendency to veer left or right as you run down the straights it's an indication you need to measure the tire stagger. The stagger may have changed because of changing air pressure or from the heating and cooling cycles of racing.

As a rule it usually is not necessary to adjust tire stagger on an asphalt track once the kart is set up. In dirt racing stagger may be changed from race to race, but this is not usually so on pavement. For more on stagger for dirt tracks refer to the section on Dirt Track Racing.

Tire air pressure is one of those things that you will most likely want to change from heat to heat. As the track temperature changes you will need to compensate for it. If it's 20 degrees hotter by the time your race is grided, you would want to increase the air pressure a couple of pounds to reduce bite. Likewise if it cools off considerably you would want to reduce air pressure to get more bite. Fine tuning is an on going thing. If you want to stay up front you have to stay one step ahead of the competition. Don't forget they're trying to stay one step ahead of you.

THE RACE

When it comes to the race itself there is little left to do. About all you can do is compensate for track and weather conditions. How many times have we said that. During the race if all is not well, you should try an analyze the situation so you can make corrections for the next heat.

58

Between races time is at a premium, especially if your running 4-cycles and need to change oil and check for a broken dipper. A few minutes more for changing a gear or adjusting a clutch, leaves precious little time for chassis adjustments. What you can do on race day is almost always controlled by the time you have to do it. At this point it's best to keep changes to small increments unless you have a serious handling problem. The only things you will have time to do is adjust tire air pressure, adjust stagger, tire track, weight bias and perhaps spindle height. These same five steps we started with sometime ago. Except now you know what to do to help. For more detailed information go back and read the appropriate sections of this book. I have also condensed this information onto a single sheet, which you may elect to carry with you to the track as a handy reference guide. I carry one with me even after all these years. Sometimes in the excitement of the day and two or three friends trying to tell you what you should do, it's easy to get off the track.

For dirt racing, things are a little more complicated because we also have to adjust for ever changing track conditions. You not only have to adjust for what happened in the last race, you have to anticipate what is going to happen in the next. Because of the complexity involved, I have included a special chapter on dirt racing.

RAINY DAYS

More and more tracks or, perhaps I should really say street races, are racing rain or shine. Rain tires are a must in these cases, and usually are required for safety. Keep the tire pressure at a reasonable level, 15 to 20 pounds rear. 10 to 15 in the front to keep the tire contact patch as big as possible and still keep the water channels open. If it's unusually cool you can reduce the pressure a few more pounds. True rain tires will wear fast if the track dries out. Try and stay in the wet areas to keep the tires cool.

Do all your braking and accelerating with the kart in a straight line. If there are any bumps, dips or what have you, try to hit them head on. A neutral kart with little or no stagger will work best.

There is an opportunity to practice in the rain or wet which most karters fail to take advantage of. At least two or three times a year you will have a rainy day at your local club races. Most all tracks allow karts to go out and dry off the track. This is a good time to find out how your kart handles on a wet track. You can get a feel for the handling under braking, which is perhaps the most important part of driving in the rain.

If you switch to rain tires for this effort don't stay out until the track is dry or you will burn up a lot of good rubber. Rain tires do not wear well on a dry track. For more information on rain tires refer to the section on tires.

INDOOR RACING

Indoor racing presents a different set of circumstances to kart handling. Most tracks are small and on very smooth concrete. Most promoters have taken to spraying the track with Coke syrup or brake fluid to improve traction.

To do well in this type of racing you need to keep the kart tight. There is a lot of pushing and bumping so it's very important to keep the kart down tight so a competitor can't get under you and nudge you out of the way.

Left turn only and offset chassis karts work well under these circumstances because of the additional left side weight. Most tracks are near circular so you can run lots of stagger.

If you can make your kart handle on the outside, you can quite often pass a train of karts battling it out in the inside groove. The only problem is that many of the slower karts in the inside get shoved to the outside. Almost anyone that gets spun out will spin into the outside lane. If you handle good outside, it's sometimes best to lay back a bit and let the field sort itself out before you make your move. That's assuming you have enough laps to do that.

DIRT TRACKS

Dirt racing is a whole different type of racing than asphalt racing. The biggest difference is the ever changing track conditions, from mud, to hard packed clay, to dust, and it can all happen in the same night.

Dirt racing offers much the same classes as asphalt racing but there is more of a distinction between the lower powered Briggs classes and the high power classes, such as open Briggs and 2-cycle classes. It's almost entirely two different types of racing requiring different driving styles and kart setup.

In the classes such as stock Briggs, the dirt tracks require all the same precision and care in regards to chassis setup as pavement racing. In the more powerful classes, where you have some horsepower to play with, you can be a little less perfect and still win. Having enough horsepower to power slide around the corners is a good feeling.

If it is your first time at a dirt track, take the time to watch and see how the other competitors in your class are driving the track. You will see some hot shoes running down into the corner, flip the kart into a power slide and then stand hard on the accelerator. In the higher horsepower classes you will need to do that, but in most Briggs classes that is not the fast way around the track. Even in dirt racing, as hectic as it seems, the adage, "Keep it smooth", still applies. Even more so in the lower horsepower restricted classes.

It is imperative that the kart chassis is set up initially so that you can keep a handle on the amount of changes you will need to make at the track. In asphalt racing, after you have the kart dialed in you may only need to adjust tire air pressure throughout the day, while with dirt tracks more effort is required to keep ahead of changing track conditions.

The most difficult aspect of dirt racing is the ever changing track conditions. Tracks come in all kinds of surfaces and they all progress through several different changes throughout the evening. Some start out as a couple of inches of mud and end up as hard as cement and rougher than heck. The really successful dirt racers are able to read these ever changing conditions and compensate for them. While horsepower is always important, it is no good if you can't get the power to the ground. It is essential to keep the chassis planted to the ground, and working for you, not against you.

Dirt racing is whole different type of racing than asphalt racing. Every track is different and in some cases every corner is different. Dirt racing is not for everyone but for some its the only way to go.

TRACK SURFACES

The key to successful dirt racing is to have a reasonably good handling kart when you arrive at the track and having the ability to judge what the track will do. Reading the track, as it is called, is important as the track surface will change from heat to heat and again for the feature. Being able to anticipate how the track will be, when it's your time to race is the real key to success.

Most track operators grade and wet down the track before the days program. For this reason most tracks start out wet and muddy, then become spongy and progress to hard and rutty. If you keep changing your setup for the progression, you can stay close to the proper setup.

The rate at which the track changes depends on many things. The material that makes up the track surface, weather conditions, the number of karts using the track and whether or not the track is watered again before the features.

If the track is watered before the feature, it then becomes important whether you are racing early or late in the rotation. The first couple of features will have to plan on a gummy, softer track. The last couple of features will have to plan on a hard surface and perhaps, if there are a lot of karts, some rubber.

62

Track surfaces usually fall into one of four categories; Muddy, Tacky, sometimes called wet slick, Dry slick, and Dusty. I will try to give you some idea of how to read a track as it changes, so you will have some idea of the changes that will need to be made between races. Just remember, nobody knows it all. You will learn something new each week. If you make the effort, you should find yourself improving every week.

MUDDY

A muddy track is one that splatters your kart, helmet, everything in sight with globs of mud. Most tracks don't stay this way very long. Unless you race early in the rotation, you may be able to avoid this type of track.

A muddy wet track is probably the most beneficial to the under powered karters. This track surface is usually the result of a recent rain or a watering down of the track by the management. Muddy tracks are usually encountered in early practice sessions. Usually they turn tacky by race time. Widen the chassis out both front and rear. More inside weight will help you come off the corners straighter. Use treaded tires. A rectangular tread design will work better than the straight grooves. The deeper the grooves the better. On a 2-cycle, a larger tire can be used. A little more tire pressure can be used since your getting as much bite as the track will allow. High corner entry will help keep you low on the track through the corners and let the kart drift back out coming off the corner. Try not to break the tires loose as you'll spin yourself out. Horsepower is almost useless. Feather the throttle in the corners and actually do the steering with the throttle. Jerking the wheel will only result in you losing control. Stagger isn't as important here. Too much stagger will be hard to control down the straight.

TACKY

A tacky track all but sucks your shoes off when walking across it. The heel of your shoe will indent the track easily, Treaded tires will mark the surface. Tacky is probably the best condition for a race track to be in, although not the fastest condition. Tacky tracks suck up horsepower and require a lot of gear because the tires will get such good grip on the track. The kart will be easy to drive. Treaded or grooved tires are still the best choice here. Narrowing the front end, especially moving the right front in should help. Moving the left rear in tight, and the right rear out to the end of the axle is a good starting point. This will make the kart feel more stable down the straight and come off the corners very straight.

The quick line should be a wide corner entry with late apex, down low in the corner and keep RPM up through the corner. Drive straight off the lowest part of the straight. Make an oval track into a circular one. Low entry into turns should only be made to protect position, as this is where most passing will occur. Stagger is probably the most important on this type of track as you want as little rolling friction and tire scrub as possible. Smaller width tires are the answer. 5.50 or 6.00 on the rears. 4.50's or smaller on the front. Grooved rears and treaded fronts are a good combination. Run more tire pressure to get a smaller foot print, less rolling friction.

When the track is heavy or wet, you want to keep the tire from rolling over and flexing the sidewall more. You don't need a lot of tire patch here because the track is very sticky. More air pressure is used on wet/heavy tracks to decrease tire patch.

HARD SLICK

When the track dries out, you get a smooth hard slick surface. It may even develop a groove from tire rubber laid down in the racing grove. When the groove get hard and clean, dust and loose stuff gets blown to the outside, typically a one groove race track, it's time to change to slicks.

At most dirt tracks you will find a wide variety of karts. This one has the motor mounted in the rear and to the left side. This type works best with high horse power engines, however, they do need front end weight to keep the front wheels on the ground.

Yes, you can and should run slicks on a track like this. The racing grove will become as hard as asphalt as the night wears on. Start out with a soft tire. For the 4-cycle classes stay small on the rears, say 5.50 or 6.00's you may want to try a 5.50 on the right front or even both fronts of the kart if a push develops. After the tires build heat and really stick well, check that they are not overheating, collecting excessive rubber buildup or shredding the inside edges. The harder and slicker, the track becomes the more you need to go down on tire air pressure. Less air pressure creates more tire patch, which in turn gives better tire grip. Lower air pressure is used in situations where more bite is required, or bite is hard to get. 4 or 5 pounds in the left rear is not uncommon. 6 to 8 is not unheard of for the right rear either. I've seen right rear's roll under on 2-cycles, however I don't believe this is desirable. On the front keep a little harder at say 8 to 10 pounds. As tires start to overheat or wear poorly, go to a harder compound. As far as set-up, tuck the right rear closer to the frame rails as the track gets harder and slicker. Moving the left rear out will help transfer weight to the right rear. Keep the front fairly narrow with the left front in a bit tighter than the right front.

Hard slick tracks also have a tendency to become very rough. About like an asphalt track with pot holes, of course the pot holes are always in the middle of the fast lane. When a track holds moisture all night, it will invariably become rough as the track will work and move around under the strains of karts trying to make straight lines out of the turns. A bumpy track only gets worse as the night goes on. If a hole or rut can be avoided then by all means do it, but often times the fast line is through all the bumps, so you have to adjust to this track surface. Set the kart similar to a tacky track, however run lower tire pressures. Use a little taller gear. Keep the right rear out a ways so as to prevent bicycling through the ruts. 10-15 lbs. is good all around.

LATE NIGHT SLICK

This is a condition which occurs in the fall of the year in the midwest. Moisture will seep back up

out of the racing surface producing a shiny slick surface. You can tell this is happening to the track, as you will see beads of water collecting on your tow vehicle and tool boxes.

This is probably the most difficult track to hook up on. Often parts of the track are dry and hard while a low spot or poorly lit area will be wet on the surface. This wetness cleans the tires right off as you drive through and you'll inevitably lose traction. Slicks may be the quick way around 3/4 of the track but once on the wet slick portion you'll be on the edge of control. Treaded tires are the choice for lesser experienced drivers. You won't give up much through the hard dry and you'll have a better grip on things through the wet spots. Often grooved slicks are the best all around choice here. I prefer a soft compound, 6.00 or 6.50 on the rear with hand cut grooves to get around the quickest. Try to travel over the wet spots in a straight line if possible.

Note on grooving, 2 or 3 circumference grooves should be cut on the rears with a few cross grooves. The number is dependent on the condition of the track surface. Fronts should have only circumference grooves as forward bite is not needed. The more wet the track, the more grooves you'll want. The tackier or drier the track becomes, the less grooves. For more information on grooving refer to the chapter on tires.

DUSTY

Dust bowl conditions, no hardened surface. Common in low clay areas with sandy soil. Kart set-up will be much the same as a muddy track, although tire selection will be better with grooved tires or slicks with a few cuts in them. Some grooving is necessary to route the loose stuff out from under the tires rather than the tires sliding over the track surface. Try to stay low on the track as loose stuff blows to the outside edges of the track. You may even find a cushion right at the edge of the groove. You can ride right on the side of the cushion but don't break through it into the loose stuff above the groove, or the back end will come right on around.

DIRT KART SETUP

If you don't make changes as the night goes along, you'll be left behind in the first turn. You should always be doing something to the chassis throughout the night.

You want the kart to be as wide as possible without giving up bite. Don't start out wide and move in. Instead start out in tight and work out until the kart becomes loose. As the track dries out, the kart will loosen up. You should correct this by tucking in the right rear. Also, as a track dries out, it becomes inherently faster. You should be dropping teeth on the rear gear throughout the night. Decreasing stagger also helps as a track dries. If the rear is still loose you can drop the left front spindle, this will put more weight on the right rear.

A flexible kart works best on dirt. Rubber grommets, nylon inserts and the like are common place between all mounted components to achieve the most flex possible. The most critical items are seat mounting, floor pan, bumpers and nerf bars. Rather than letting the bumpers and nerf bars flop around, it is safer to mount them in rubber or plastic bushings. A good method of floor pan installation is using a dab of silicone between frame tabs and the pan. Be sure to drill each mounting hole oversize in the above components. I use 1/4" bolts through 5/16" holes. Use locking nuts but don't tighten completely.

STAGGER

Adjusting stagger is perhaps the most common adjustment made throughout the night. How do you create various amounts of stagger at the track? The only real answer is to mount up all the tires you have and measure them. If you have a lot of extra wheels laying around mount several different tires, even different brands. Stagger can only be changed in small degrees by increasing or reducing air pressure. Each tire has a predetermined size and it's difficult to adjust the size a great deal. The easiest way to adjust tire size is by changing rim widths, which is best done at home.

You can run more stagger on oval tracks. The smaller the track the more stagger you can run. On 1/10 mile soup bowl tracks you can run 3 to 4 inches, especially if there is any degree of banking. For tracks that are larger or flatter less stagger is required. Wet and tacky tracks require less stagger. As the track dries and becomes harder, use more stagger.

The camber on this kart is of some interest. You may be able to get the right front to make good contact with the track, but the left front will never be in a acceptable position.

TIRE TRACK

If the kart has a pushing problem the type of adjustment to be made depends on where the push takes place. If the kart is pushing going into a turn, the kart is too tight on the right rear. Space the right rear wheel out, or take some right rear weight out of the kart. Move some weight to the front. Another thing you can do is add more stagger.

If the kart is loose coming off a turn this is indicative of having too much stagger. Decrease stagger. If the kart is loose on a dry/slick track, the kart needs more rear weight. Add it evenly to the rear end. Raising up the nose of the kart (adjusting the spindles down) will add more weight to the rear.

Other adjustments which can be made to compensate for a pushing or loose condition is to adjust the front and rear track of the kart. At the front, the front wheels can be moved in or out with different wheel offsets. At the rear, the wheels can be spaced in or out along the axle. For instance, if the race track starts out wet and tacky, a racer might start with his chassis setup with the front and rear track widths equal. As the track dries out, he can move the right rear in. For an extremely dry slick track, he would probably move the right rear all the way in and maybe change to a smaller offset wheel for the right front to reduce the front track width.

DIRT DRIVING TECHNIQUE

A lot of karters like to setup their karts so they will work best in the last few laps of a race. You have to be very careful if you are doing this. You can't afford to let the race get away from you. This is not big time sprint racing like you see on television, where they have lots of power available. Most kart engines are relatively close in power and there is little to spare. If you are starting in the middle of the pack, or in the front half, and have about the same power as the karters ahead of you, you need to make a move early, in the first couple of laps. In this case, you want your kart handling pretty good right off the bat. I personally believe that the best time to make a move is in the first lap or two. Later in the race when things are spread out, if the handling starts to change, you can make minor adjustments in your driving style to compensate for handling changes, but when the field is bunched up, you don't have room or time to be adjusting your driving style. You want everything to be just right. I prefer my kart just a little loose, so I endeavor to start the race with the kart setup for very little or no push. Then as the track dries, the kart will become looser, just about the time the traffic is thinning out, and I can let the tail hang out a little.

This kart has the rear torison bar set for maximum stiffness. Note, the home made tire pattern. Dirt drivers will do anything for more bite.

The right front spindle height is adjustable from the drivers seat on this kart.

If you are starting in the rear, but feel you have more power than most of your fellow competitors, you can lay back for a lap or two and wait for the field to spread out a bit, and pick them off one at a time. In this case, you can set your kart up to work best later in the race. To be honest though, in most of the features I've seen, most of the passing is done in the first four or five laps and the rest of the race is mostly a follow the leader deal.

If you are running a class with a lot of horsepower, you can use the throttle to transfer weight to the front or rear. Letting up on the throttle transfers weight to the front, while applying throttle transfers weight to the rear. Careful testing will allow you to judge precisely how this actually effects your kart so you can make slight adjustments while driving. This could help you on a track that changes during the main event. This is next to impossible to do with a stock Briggs because of its limited horsepower.

If you have a kart with front spindles, adjustable from the seat ,you can make some adjustments during the race. As a track changes from tacky to hard more bite will be necessary. You usually want more weight transfer. The left front spindle should be adjusted downward as the track hardens. This forces the right rear to bite.

The little knob just to the left of the driver seat is to enable the driver to adjust the frame flex during the race.

When making spindle changes remember that when the spindle is moved up, the front of the kart is lowered, and when the spindle is lowered, the front of the kart is raised.

Lowering the left front spindle will increase the weight on the right rear. Raising the left front spindle will increase the weight on the left rear Lowering the right front spindle will increase the weight on the left rear. Raising the right front spindle will increase the weight on the right rear.

If your kart allows you to adjust the frame flex during the race you can change the kart handling to compensate for changing track conditions. By stiffening the frame you reducing flex which will remove bite from the right rear which will reduce bicycling or hopping. This will also help to over come a pushing or understeer condition. By adjusting the frame to be more flexable you can transfer more weight to the right rear. This will improve rear bite which will help over come a loose or oversteering condition.

In the higher horsepower classes, some karters like to set the weight bias heavy on the right side. They drive into the corner harder, set the kart for the corner, twitch the steering wheel, and then use the throttle to bring the kart out of the turn. This broadsliding method is very common in high horsepower classes.

If you are having difficulty learning to slide the rear into the corners, try running with the rear end set wide. You can also over inflate the rear tires or use more offset in the rims. It is best to practice this in a practice session. You may only want to try this setup until you become comfortable with broadsliding the kart through the turns. As you get on to it, you will find that it is relatively easy, and should only require a simple left, right turning of the steering wheel. If you find yourself over correcting more than this, you are probably correcting for a poor handling kart or an improper driving style.

If you get into a race and find you have a bad push, you can compensate for it by using the following driving technique. You can force the front to bite more by applying the brakes while the steering wheel is in a turned position. When you apply the brakes in a turning mode, do it with a sharp jabbing motion. This will transfer weight from the rear end onto the front. The front end should start to bite, acting a lot like front wheel brakes. This transfers weight to the front and the rear end becomes very light. The net result is that the back end will want to continue going forward while the front end wants to turn. When the rear end breaks loose, you will have changed the handling from a pushing condition to a loose condition. You can then drive the kart out of the turn with the throttle. Granted, this is not a good situation, and you will not be very fast but at least you will be able to finish the race. As a rule, you should never brake while turning unless you are trying to avoid an accident, but in this case it's the only alternative.

Circumference grooves are used on the front to increase traction and help steering.

To get the most benfit from the angle cut. The angle should be square to the track when the kart is positioned as it will be during most of the race.

As a track dries out it may be necessary to try different things. Its not uncommon for dirt racer to switch to slicks as the track becomes harder.Note, the tires are mounted close in for more bite.

BABY KARTS

If you are not familiar with the baby karts, they are about 3/4 the size of the adult karts and are powered by 50cc Coomer engines. This class is still in its infancy so we can expect alot of rule changes for the first couple of years.

The baby karts are a fine addition to the field of karting. They allow the five and six year old kids a chance to learn the feel of competition and to hone their driving abilities before they develop that win at all cost attitude.

Making a baby kart handle properly is just as important as setting up a full size kart. May be not so much as for speed, but for making the kart comfortable and safe to drive. The biggest problem is educating the kids enough that they can tell you what is happening on the track.

Most kids at this age will not push the kart to the limit. They will drive at a pace that is comforable for them. As soon as the kart begins to get a little squirrelly or understeers the child will lift their foot from the accelerator or even step on the brake. The goal of the father is to keep raisng that comfort level so the lap times will continune to decrease.

Perhaps the most important thing for the father to do at this point in his son or daughter's career is to instill in the kid that he should be as smooth as possible. The father should incourage the kid to watch other races so he can learn the fastest groove around the track. Usually walking the track before the races will enable him to see the rubber groove used by other competitors.

The role of the pit crew, especially the father, is more important in this class than any other in karting. They need to observe how the kart and kid is behaving on the track. There are many signs to watch for if you know what you are looking for.

When the kart goes out on the track, the father's job is just beginning. For the first couple of laps watching the kids hands on the steering wheel will give you some clues. He or she should not be twitch the steering wheel back and forth in the corners. If the child is doing this we must find out the reason. The reason for doing this may be difficult to pin point, but hopfully we can sort it out by devoting our attention to the kart itself. The most common problem in kart handling, just as in the adult classes, is understeer. The kart want to go

69

The baby karts are the newest class in karting. This is something the sport can really use. A true starting place for the youngters. I hope the sanctioning bodies keep it a true stock class.

straight instead of turning. If the kart is always riding up high in the corners, and it appears as though the kid can not turn, the kart down into the apex of the turn the kart is most likely understeering. The first step in solving this problem is to reduce the front tire air pressure. If that doesn't help it may be necessary to add some front weight.

If you notice the child is always clipping the inside edge of the track, the kart may be oversteering. If this is the case, you should increase the front tire air pressure, or remove some front end weight if possible.

If the rear of the kart is swinging out on both left and right corners, more rear bite is needed. You can reduce rear tire air pressure, adjust the rear tire track in closer or if necessary add rear weight. If the problem is only on left or right hand turns, you need to adjust the outside tire on that corner of the kart.

Another thing to watch is the tires. You can tell a little about the air pressure by watching how they react in the corners. The two most obvious symptons are over and under inflation. If the tire is really low on air pressure you will see the tire roll on cornering. If the tire shows wear on the outer

The Baby kart class features a short 32" wheelbase kart powered by a 50cc Commer engine.

A pack of young lions eagerly awaiting their turn on the track.

edges, (rounding of the outer edge of the tire), you are probably four or five pounds light. Over inflation is best recognized by the appearance of a narrow band wearing down the center of the tire. One simple method to highlight what is happening is to run a couple of chalk marks across the tire from one side to the other. Run the kart a few laps or a heat race and observe what has happened to the chalk marks. The results should correspond to the condition mentioned above.

One point of variation between baby karts is in the selection of tire size. I have seen both 3.00 and 4.50 inch tires being used on the front of some baby karts. The theory all says that the narrow tires should work best. They have less frontal drag and are some what easier to steer. However, if the kart has a problem with understeer, not wanting to turn, the bigger tires may help. Understeer should first be attacked using conventional methods such as adding front end weight and adjusting tire track. If understeer is still a problem, the larger tire patch of the bigger tire may be necessary.

Since the youngster has no experience to work with and really doesn't know how the kart should

A field of Baby karts awaiting the green flag. Currently the baby kart races are being started from a standing start. This eliminates any confusion about the starting order.

feel, it's up to the father to check out the kart between races. One important thing he should check is the front end for binding. Check the tie-rods with the steering at lock each way and insure the tie rods are loose and not bound up. It's also a good idea to give the rear axle a spin to insure the chain and wheel bearings are free. Another important point is to insure that the brakes are working properly.

It's a good idea to let the child become involved in the karting effort. Most kids can do things like oil the chain, clean his helmet visor, and go around and make sure all the tires have air in them. As they get older you can add task such as measuring tire air pressure and adding fuel. Don't forget to leave some free time. Kids should have some time to just be a kid.

At this point in their career I hope the kids and their father don't loose sight of the fact that they are supose to go out and have fun. All too soon they will grow into the advance classes where running up front becomes so much more important.

Don't overlook the fact that all the material presented in the book for full size karts also apply to Baby karts. Things like weight distribution and front end alignment are just as important to good handling no matter the size of the kart.

Appendix

I have included a few items which I felt you may be able to make use of. The Quick Fix Handling Reference Guide, Chassis Baseline Worksheet, and the Weight Distribution Worksheet have been positioned so you can tear them out and make copies without destorying the book.

Karting Terms

Ackerman steering: Ackerman steering is where the inside front wheel is steered in a sharper arc than the outside front wheel.

Angle of Attack: The angle of attack is the number of degrees the trailing edge of the wing is above the leading edge of the wing. As the angle of attack is increased, down force is increased. However, drag is also increased.

Baseline: Is a detailed layout of exactly how the kart was setup initially.

Bicycling: The kart has a tendency to lift the two inside tires off the ground during cornering.

Camber: The inward or outward tilt of the wheel at the top when compared with the contact patch. If the top of the wheel tilts inward toward the kart, the camber is negative.

Caster: Is the angle forward or rearward from vertical that the spindle is mounted on the front axle. Caster is best viewed from the side of the kart.

Caster Stagger: Caster stagger occures when the right and left spindles are adjusted for different caster angles. This is more common in dirt racing than pavement racing.

Darting: Darting is defined as a kart that twitches or darts at the slightest movement of the steering wheel. Darting is most often caused by improper toe-in setting.

Drag: Drag is any kind of resistance to the forward movement of the kart. There are three kinds of drag, form drag, friction drag, and induced drag.

Durometer: Is a instrument used to measure the hardness of a tire compound.

Enduro Karts: Enduro karts are a lower more streamlined style kart. The driver is in a reclinded position to improve streamlining. Enduros get their name from the fact they run timed events on tracks such as Mid-Ohio, Daytona, and Charlotte.

Friction Drag: Is the drag caused by air friction as the air moves in and around all the protrusions on the kart.

Form Drag: Form drag is the drag caused by the turbulence which is present in the area immediately following the kart.

Grooving: Grooving is the removal of rubber from a tire in such a way as to make grooves. This can be done to slicks to obtain more bite. Dirt tires can also be grooved to increase the number of blocks.

Induced Drag: Induced drag is the drag caused by adding wings and spoilers to the kart.

Kingpin: The kingpin is the pivot around which the spindle rotates. The king pin bolt is the large bolt which mounts the spindle to the spindle bracket welded to the front axle.

Kingpin Inclination: The kingpin inclination is the angle between the king pin axis and a true vertical line drawn from where the king pin axis hits the ground.

LTO: Refers to karts maded for oval or speedway racing. LTO is a acronym for Left Turn Only.

Oversteer: Is when the front bite of the kart is so good the kart darts into the turn. In most cases this causes the rear of the kart to brake loose and usually causes a spin out.

Pyrometer: Is a instrument used to measure tire temperatures. Tire temperatures can tell you if the kart handling is adjusted properly.

Rear Steer: Rear steer is when the rear axle position is shifted slightly forward or rearward on one side of the kart. The perpose being to help steer the kart into the corner.

Shifter Karts: Shifter karts generally have 125cc engines with a gearbox. They run on the larger kart tracks and at most street races.

Side Bite: Side bite is a term which refers to the ability of the kart to stay stuck to the track when cornering.

Siping: It the cutting of razor cuts or slits into the blocks of a dirt tire. Siping tends to give a tire a bit more bite.

Stagger: The difference in tire circumference from one side of the kart to another. In oval racing the inside tires are smaller than the outside.

Stall: Is the point when a wings angle of attack is so great the turbulence of the air causes so much drag that there is no gain in down force.

Tire Compound: The compound of the tire is the composition of the rubber making up the tire. The compound determines if the tire is soft (wears fast), or hard (long lasting).

Tire Track: Tire track is the distance between the tires across the width of the kart. Not the karts wheelbase.

Toe-In: Is the effect of having the front edges of the tires closer together than the corresponding point at the rear edge of the tires. This effect tends to offset the tendency of the kart to wander.

Torsion Bar: Any bar or brace which is mounted in such a way as to exert force upon a frame member. Any long tube can be a torsion bar. A kart hurling into a corner creates a lot of force, enough to flex most any tube. The key is to control the amount of flex.

Understeer: Is plowing, or when the kart doesn't go where you want it to. The kart tries to continue in a straight line.

Wheel Offset: The offset of a wheel is measured from the wheel center to the inner edge of the rim.

QUICK FIX
HANDLING REFERENCE GUIDE

TIRE STAGGER

1. A larger tire will always try to turn around a smaller tire.
2. Stagger can be changed by changing tire sizes or tire air pressure.
3. Stagger can be set front and rear.
4. The amount of turning force is controlled by the amount of stagger.
5. Increasing stagger makes the kart more loose.
6. Decreasing stagger makes a kart tighter, more likely to push.

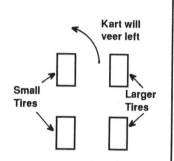

SPINDLE ADJUSTMENT

1. If kart is understeering Lower chassis, raise spindle in bracket.
2.. Lowering spindle transfers more weight to opposite rear corner
3. If kart is oversteering Raise shassis, lower spindle in bracket.
4. Raising spindle transfers more weight to rear on the same side

**Higher Spindle
Lower Chassis**

**Lower Spindle
Higher Chassis**

GENERAL NOTES

1. Track has lots of corners use wide track.
2. Track has few corners use narrow track.
3. Lots of left and right turns, little or no stagger.
4. Lots of straight-a-ways, no stagger.
5. Oval track lots of stagger.

FOR RAIN

1. Make front & rear track narrower
2. Use narrower front & rear tires or rims
3. Increase air pressure
4. Brake only in a straight line.

QUICK FIX
HANDLING REFERENCE GUIDE

CHASSIS PERFORMANCE

If kart is loose in rear	If kart is pushing (Won't turn)
Oversteer	**Understeer**

1. Wider front track	1. Narrower front track
2. Narrower front tires	2. Wider front tires
3. Harder front tires	3. Softer front tires
4. Narrower rear track	4. Wider rear track
5. Wider rear tires	5. Narrower rear tires
6. Softer compound rear tires	6. Harder compound rear tires
7. Higher air pressure in front	7. Lower air pressure in front
8. Lower air pressure in rear	8. Higher air pressure in rear
9. Move weight to rear	9. Move weight to front
10. Decrease stagger	10. Increase stagger
11. Loosen rear bumper	11. Tighten rear bumper
12. Increase frame flex	12. Decrease frame flex

AIR PRESSURE

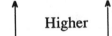

Higher	Lower
1. Less bite (Looser)	1. More bite
2. Reduce bicycleing	2. Reduce loose condition
3. Less sidewall flex	3. More sidewall flex
4. Tire will wear in center	4. Tire wears on outside edges
5. Same effect as a harder tire compound	5. Same effect as softer tires

TRACK WIDTH

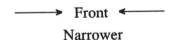

Front Narrower

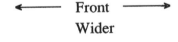

Front Wider

Front Narrower	Front Wider
1. Front will bite more	1. Front will less more
2. Steer easier	2. Steer harder
3. Transfer less weight	3. Transfer more weight
4. Rear will bite less	4. Rear will bite more

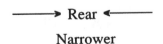

Rear Narrower

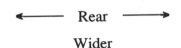

Rear Wider

Rear Narrower	Rear Wider
1. Rear will bite more	1. Rear will bite less
2. Front will bite less(push more)	2. Front will bite more (less push)

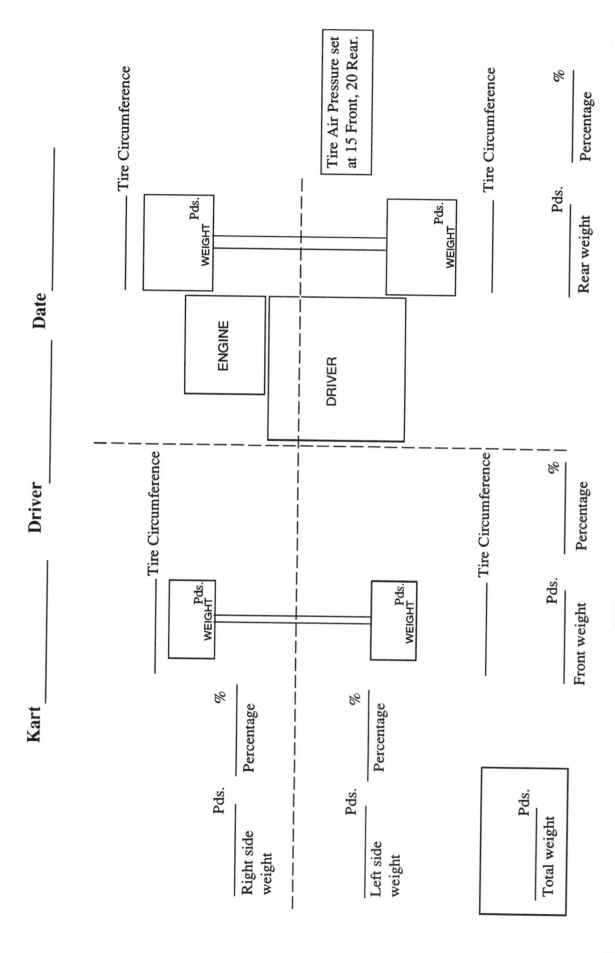

WEIGHT DISTRIBUTION WORKSHEET

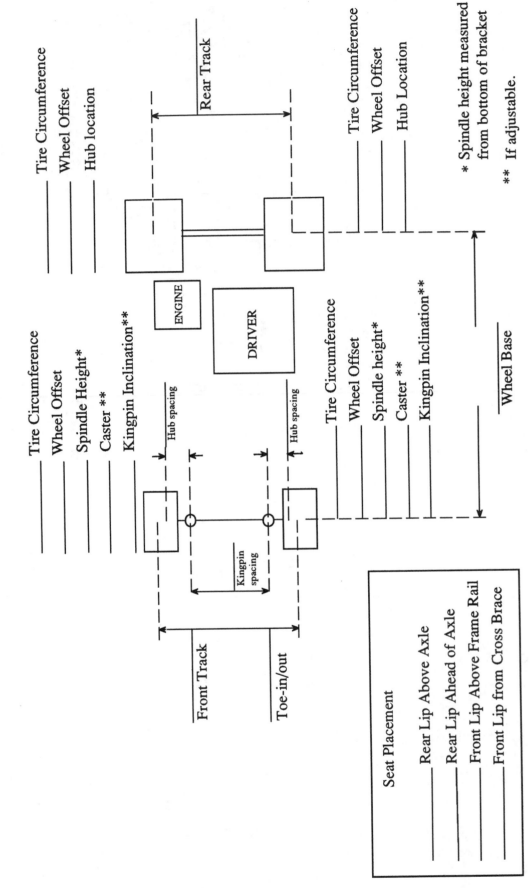

Kart _____

Date _____

Tire Circumference _____
Wheel Offset _____
Spindle Height* _____
Caster ** _____
Kingpin Inclination** _____

Hub spacing

ENGINE

DRIVER

Tire Circumference _____
Wheel Offset _____
Spindle height* _____
Caster ** _____
Kingpin Inclination** _____

Hub spacing

Kingpin spacing

Front Track

Toe-in/out

Tire Circumference _____
Wheel Offset _____
Hub location _____

Rear Track

Tire Circumference _____
Wheel Offset _____
Hub Location _____

* Spindle height measured from bottom of bracket

** If adjustable.

Wheel Base

CHASSIS BASELINE WORKSHEET

Seat Placement

_____ Rear Lip Above Axle
_____ Rear Lip Ahead of Axle
_____ Front Lip Above Frame Rail
_____ Front Lip from Cross Brace

Index

Martin Motorsports Publications

Competitive Karting $12.95 Plus S&H

A comprehensive guide for the individual who is seriously considering entering the karting field. Complete information on, how to begin, what to buy, and how to prepare a kart for racing. Everything you need to know to be competitive in your very first race. This book offers detailed information never before available to the beginning karter. Here's your chance to gain the competitive edge! You don't have to be a spectator anymore. Karting can put you in the drivers seat where you can experience the thrill of victory first hand. Order your copy today. Only $12.95 plus $1.50 Shipping and handling.

4-Cycle Kart Engines $9.95 Plus S&H

A guide to all 4-cycle engines used in karting today. Also includes chapters on camshafts and computers in karting. A very good book for the rookie karter who really wants basic stock information. This book can get you started on the right foot in the engine department. Order today only $9.95 plus $1.50 shipping and handling.

Karting Tools & Tips $9.95 Plus S&H

Now a book that can save you time and money. Over 125 karting related tools and ideas you can use every day. You don't have to buy a lot of expensive tools to be a competitive karter. You won't beleive the number of labor saving devices lying right under your nose. Karting can be fun and enjoyable. Let Martin Motorsports help you find the way. Order this fine book today. You'll be glad you did. Only $9.95 plus $1.50 shipping and handling.

All books are 8 1/2 x 11, soft cover. These are well prepared, well written books, not copy machine copies. You can be proud to add them to your karting library.

MARTIN MOTORSPORTS

P. O. BOX 12654   FT WAYNE, IND. 46864